OAKLEY
LIFEBOATS

An Illustrated History of the RNLI's
Oakley and Rother Lifeboats

OAKLEY LIFEBOATS

An Illustrated History of the RNLI's Oakley and Rother Lifeboats

Nicholas Leach

TEMPUS

Wells' 37ft Oakley *Ernest Tom Neathercoat* launching on exercise. (Eastern Counties Newspapers, by courtesy of Paul Russell)

First published 2003

PUBLISHED IN THE UNITED KINGDOM BY:
Tempus Publishing Ltd
The Mill, Brimscombe Port
Stroud, Gloucestershire GL5 2QG

PUBLISHED IN THE UNITED STATES OF AMERICA BY:
Tempus Publishing Inc.
2 Cumberland Street
Charleston, SC 29401

British Library Cataloguing in Publication Data.
A catalogue record for this book is available from the British Library.

ISBN 0 7524 2784 9

Typesetting and origination by Tempus Publishing.
Printed in Great Britain by Midway Colour Print, Wiltshire.

Contents

Acknowledgements

Many people have assisted with this book, in particular Jeff Morris, who provided information and photographs; Tony Denton, who checked through the after-service information and supplied many photographs; and Derek Scrivener at RNLI Head-quarters, who supplied movement information on the individual lifeboats. Others kindly supplied photographs for possible inclusion, and in particular I am grateful to: Paul Russell; David Phillipson; Tony Denton; Colin Watson; Paul Arro; W.F. Flett; Tony Moore; Derek Page; Richard Martin; Mark Roberts; Graham Taylor; John Markham; Brian Grenfell; Tony Smith and Michael Welch. Photographs are credited individually. Mention must also be made of the late Mike Searle, who provided many stimulating comments and constructive criticisms of the original work, and I am sure he would have enjoyed this edition. I am grateful to Edward Wake-Walker and staff at the RNLI's Public Relations Department for providing research facilities at RNLI HQ, Poole, and enabling the late Grahame Farr's meticulous records to be consulted. A book such as this, containing much factual information, is likely to contain some errors – they are the responsibility of the author alone. Lastly, on a personal note, my thanks to Sarah for all her support, help and useful ideas which improved the text.

Introduction

The lifeboat developed by, and named after, Richard Oakley, for the Royal National Lifeboat Institution (RNLI) in the 1950s, was a significant technological step forward in lifeboat design, and can be regarded as the first of the modern generation of self-righting motor lifeboats. Between 1958 and 1972, twenty-six Oakley lifeboats were constructed. In the 1970s the design was developed further when the 37ft 6in Rother, with the same hull shape as the Oakley but with improved crew protection, was introduced. For more than three decades, Oakley and Rother lifeboats gave excellent service throughout the United Kingdom and Republic of Ireland and performed many outstanding rescues. This book is intended to be a complete record of the Oakley and Rother lifeboats and is divided into three parts. Part One examines the historical background to the self-righting lifeboats, providing an overview of the Oakley design while tracing the evolution of the self-righting lifeboat from the eighteenth century to the present day. Part Two provides summary information about, and photographs of, the twenty-six Oakleys and fourteen Rothers built and operated by the RNLI. Part Three looks at what became of the craft after they left the RNLI's service.

1

Development of the Oakley Lifeboat

For more than two centuries the work of life-saving at sea off the coasts of the British Isles has been undertaken by volunteers using lifeboats incorporating the best contemporary technology. The Royal National Lifeboat Institution (RNLI) was founded in 1824, and since then has been responsible for funding and maintaining lifeboats and the lifeboat service. Throughout its history the RNLI has strived to find the best design of lifeboat for its crews. When the 37ft Oakley class was designed and developed during the mid-1950s, it marked a major breakthrough in lifeboat design. The first Oakley entered service in 1958, and this class of boat remained in service until the early 1990s. The Oakley design was notable for two reasons: (1) because of the unusual system of self-righting that was employed and (2) because it was the first lifeboat to have a high degree of inherent stability and yet also quickly self-right in the event of a capsize. Finding a way to combine these two, apparently opposed, elements had proved a challenge for naval architects for well over a century.

THE LIFE-BOAT ON ITS TRANSPORTING-CARRIAGE.   *To face p. 96.*

Line-drawing from the RNLI's contemporary publicity literature of the standard self-righting pulling lifeboat used almost exclusively around the coasts during the latter half of the nineteenth century. Typically, it was launched from a carriage and had high end boxes to provide sufficient buoyancy for self-righting.

The idea of a self-righting lifeboat dates back to the eighteenth century. A Frenchman, Monsieur de Bernières, invented a boat which 'would not sink when filled with water, and would not capsize when she was hove down so far that the top of her mast was immersed'. In England, in the 1780s, William Wouldhave, a parish clerk from South Shields, claimed to have built a model boat that was self-righting but his ideas were never put into practice. In 1789, the first boat specifically intended for life-saving, built by Henry Greathead of South Shields and designed by a committee in Newcastle, began operating from the mouth of the River Tyne. However it was not self-righting due to a light rockered keel, lack of buoyancy at the ends and a relatively wide beam. It was, however, the first proper design of a lifeboat and during the 1790s and 1800s, further boats of this type were built by Greathead. Although self-righting technology was apparently known in theory, it appears it was either deemed unnecessary or proved too difficult to employ in practice.

Not until the middle of the nineteenth century was a design of lifeboat incorporating the self-righting principle built in England under the influences of the RNLI and used for life-saving. Following two capsizes in the 1840s to non-self-righting lifeboats, with heavy loss of life, the need for an improved lifeboat type was evident and the idea of a self-righting lifeboat was re-examined. In 1851, Algernon, Duke of Northumberland, 'offered one hundred guineas for the best model of a Life-boat ... sent to the Surveyor's Department of the Admiralty'. The competition attracted 280 entries and, of these, that submitted by James Beeching, of Great Yarmouth, was deemed to be the best. His design was self-righting thanks to the large raised air boxes at bow and stern, the heavy iron keel and two and a half tons of water ballast.

Although Beeching's boat was deemed to be the best design submitted, it was subsequently improved by James Peake, Assistant Master Shipwright at the Royal Naval Dockyard in Woolwich. Peake's boat incorporated the better qualities of Beeching's design but was lighter and easier to manhandle on the beaches from where it would be launched. The boat built to this design at the Dockyard in 1852 was the first lifeboat used by the RNLI to employ the self-righting principle. During the subsequent trials of the boat, held at Brighton, this prototype successfully righted within five seconds of being capsized.

During the 1850s and 1860s the self-righting lifeboat was further refined and developed, and soon became the RNLI's standard type accepted and used by crews at almost every part of the coast. However, despite its widespread use, the self-righting design had a number of drawbacks. In order for it to right in the event of a capsize, it had to have high end boxes, a heavy straight keel and narrow beam, features which made it unstable when overturned, and which returned it to an upright position. However, these very features also meant it was less stable than a non-self-righting boat (in which a wider beam and greater ballast could be incorporated) and therefore it was more susceptible to capsize than its non-self-righting counterpart. To achieve a self-righting capability, some lateral stability had to be sacrificed, a fact accepted at the time by the RNLI's designers and inspectors who could not find a way to overcome the problem. Although self-righting lifeboats continued to capsize, and the lives of lifeboatmen continued to be lost, it was believed that crews using a self-righter had more chance of survival in the event of a capsize than those in a non-self-righter.

Photograph of the RNLI's standard self-righting pulling lifeboat, the mainstay of the lifeboat fleet for more than half a century. This posed photograph shows the boat on her launching carriage at a railway siding, probably on her way to her station. (From an old postcard supplied by a Shoreline member)

The benefits of self-righting were reappraised in the 1880s after the capsizing of two self-righting lifeboats on the same night in 1886 with considerable loss of life. Coupled to this appalling tragedy was the fact that an increased proportion of lifeboatmen had been lost in self-righting lifeboats over the past three decades, and this appeared to confirm the need to review the RNLI's approach to the self-righting principle once more. Before 1886, no accidents or capsizes involving a self-righter had resulted in more than half the crew being lost – indeed, most such incidents had seen the whole crew survive. However, in 1886 the worst disaster in the history of the RNLI pointed to the need for change.

On 9 December 1886, the Lytham, St Anne's and Southport lifeboats, all self-righters, were launched to the barque *Mexico*, of Hamburg, which was in distress south-west of Lytham. During the rescue, both the Southport and St Anne's lifeboats capsized. The Southport boat was found on the beach the morning after the service, when it was realised that fourteen out of her crew of sixteen had been lost. The whole crew of thirteen had been drowned from the St Anne's boat, which drifted ashore and was found bottom-up on the beach the following morning. The disaster led directly to the foundation of the Lifeboat Saturday Fund by Sir Charles Macara, which helped to raise thousands of pounds for the Institution. On the operational front, it resulted in the introduction of the Watson sailing lifeboat and a systematic and thorough review of the existing lifeboat fleet by the Institution's Inspectors.

The Watson sailing lifeboat was the result of George Lennox Watson's input into the RNLI. Watson, who was appointed Consulting Naval Architect to the Institution in 1887, produced a new lifeboat that was a significant breakthrough in lifeboat design: it had a completely different hull shape to existing designs, with greater stability incorporated into a new hull shape but sacrificing the ability to self-right. The new design, introduced in November 1890, proved popular with crews at many stations, and was widely used throughout the British Isles. With the introduction of

Watson's non-self-righting lifeboat in the 1890s, and the self-righter which remained in service, the RNLI now had two basic lifeboat designs. Both of these were used until well into the twentieth century, deployed according to local conditions and local preferences. However, the design of a fully self-righting boat that had as high a degree of stability as a non-self-righting boat was still half a century away.

In 1904 a motor lifeboat was introduced for the first time, and during the inter-war years the RNLI concentrated its building programme on the construction of powered craft. Although some lightweight self-righting motor lifeboats were built, for stations where launching across a beach was practised, the majority of motor lifeboats were based on Watson's hull shape and principles, and thus were not self-righting. These were preferred by crews, who for many years had choice of type, and consequently the popularity of the self-righter amongst lifeboatmen diminished. In 1900 the proportion of self-righting boats in the total fleet amounted to 82%. In 1920 the figure had dropped to 60%, and in 1940 was just 19%. The lowest proportion was reached in 1958 when just 2.6% of the RNLI's fleet was made up of self-righters.

In the 1950s, the RNLI's policy on self-righting boats was again reviewed after a number of lifeboats had capsized with significant loss of life to lifeboat crews. Between the end of the Second World War and 1954, five lifeboats were capsized with fatal consequences: at Mumbles (1947); Bridlington (1952); Fraserburgh (1953); Arbroath (1953) and Scarborough (1954). Tragically, these capsizes led to many lifeboatmen losing their lives and matters were made worse when the Broughty Ferry lifeboat *Mona* (ON.775) capsized in December 1959 with the loss of all eight of her crew.

The 38ft Watson sailing lifeboat *Jones-Gibb* (ON.538) which served at Barmouth from 1905 until 1939. She was one of the smaller Watsons, about 5ft shorter than her larger sister vessels, but retained the key elements of the design including a broad beam to give maximum stability. (From an old postcard supplied by a Shoreline member)

Table 1: Comparative dimensions of post-1945 carriage-launched lifeboats

	Oakley	Liverpool	Motor self-righter
Length	37ft 0in	35ft 6in	35ft 6in
Beam	11ft 6in	10ft 8in	10ft 0in
Displacement	11.16 tons	9.25 tons	9.5 tons
Water ballast	1.54 tons	0.5 tons	0.5 tons
Weight without crew or ballast	9.12 tons	8.25 tons	8.5 tons
Maximum draught loaded	38.25in	34in	35.5in
Speed	8.1kt	7.4kt	7.4kt
Endurance at full speed	140 n. miles	120 n. miles	120 n. miles
Angle of maximum stability	47 degrees	37 degrees	37 degrees
Range of stability	180 degrees	115 degrees	180 degrees

Source: *The Lifeboat*, September 1958, p.91.

A remedy was needed, but the problem of developing a stable hull which was also self-righting, had still not been overcome. The ideal was a lifeboat which was self-righting and yet retained the same lateral stability as the non-self-righting designs of Watson and his successor, James Barnett. Crews preferred boats with greater initial stability so any new design must incorporate this, as well as have the righting capability.

To ensure that a boat returns to the upright after it is forcibly turned over, three essential elements need to be built into the design: buoyancy must be kept high up in the boat; the centre of gravity needs to be low; and water must not be allowed on board when the boat is inverted. Although the self-righters were deemed to be rather poor sea boats, careful design can overcome the essential conflict between self-righting ability and seakindliness. The first design of lifeboat that overcame this

Richard Ashley, built in 1950 by Groves & Guttridge at Cowes, was stationed at Newbiggin from 1950 until 1966. She is a typical 35ft 6in Liverpool class motor lifeboat and, weighing only just over eight tons, was ideal for carriage launching. (From an old postcard supplied by a Shoreline member)

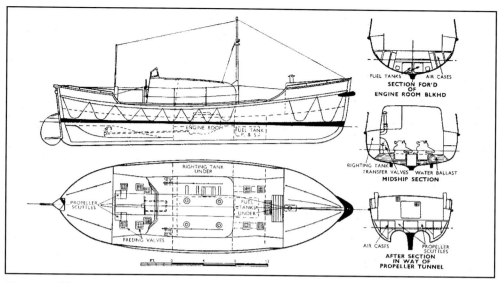

FUEL TANKS   AIR CASES
SECTION FOR'D
OF
ENGINE ROOM BLKHD

RIGHTING TANK
TRANSFER VALVES   WATER BALLAST
MIDSHIP SECTION

AIR CASES   PROPELLER
SCUTTLES
AFTER SECTION
IN WAY OF
PROPELLER TUNNEL

The general lines of the 37ft Oakley as built with open aft cockpit. The righting tank, water ballast and transfer valves are all marked in the diagram of the midship section.

conflict was the 37ft type designed by Richard Oakley in the mid-1950s. Oakley became the Consultant and Naval Architect to the RNLI in 1947 and applied himself to the problem of self-righting that had defeated his predecessors. He succeeded where others had failed by the use of an ingenious water ballast transfer system in his new 37ft design, and his ideas revolutionised lifeboat design. The boat that was subsequently built to his plans showed that the best features of both self-righting and non-self-righting boats could be incorporated into a lifeboat which was self-righting and had maximum stability when upright.

During the design process for the new lifeboat, Oakley, together with the RNLI's designers, decided that one and a half tons of water ballast was to be used in the new design to give added displacement and consequently greater stability once the boat was afloat. By allowing this to drain whilst the boat was being recovered on a beach, weight was minimised, an important consideration as the new design was intended primarily for launch and recovery off an open beach. However, the self-righting question had not been solved.

Consideration was then given to the method used by the Dutch Lifeboat Society in its larger boats, first used in the lifeboat *Insulinde* in 1927. Righting was achieved by virtue of a tank on one side which filled from the sea if the boat capsized, and caused the boat to right. Although unsuitable for the new British design, as the waterline with the boat in the overturned position would not provide sufficient immersion to fill the righting tank, the idea of transferring the water from the ballast tank to a righting tank was seen as a viable way of providing self-righting. Further investigation showed that the idea had promise and so it was pursued further.

Oakley and his designers soon realised that self-righting was possible using this method which involved the transfer of 1.54 tons of water ballast into a righting tank on the port side. The water passed through two trunks or rectangular pipes in which

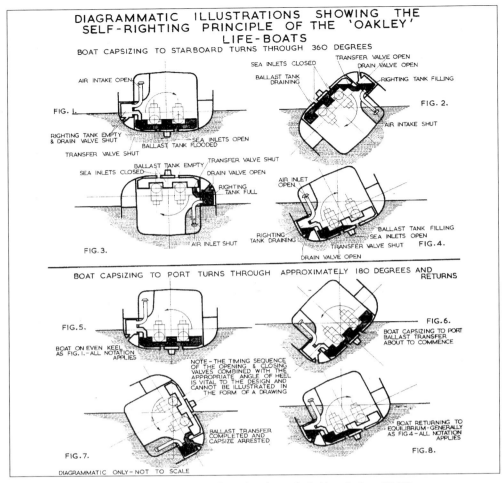

Diagrams showing the self-righting method used in the 37ft Oakley design. (RNLI)

were two valves that operated when the lifeboat was heeled over to an angle of about 110 degrees. Because of the position of the righting tanks in the hull, the lifeboat would always right the same way. Therefore, if the lifeboat capsized to starboard it would pass through 360 degrees during the righting process; but if it capsized to port it would right to port and thus only go through 180 degrees. During trials, righting took about six seconds from the overturned position to the boat being upright. The transfer of water began just before the point when the lifeboat would otherwise capsize, and so return the boat to the upright. On righting, water from the ballast tank drained into the sea while the tank refilled. Speed of righting was essential, with valves ensuring that the water was transferred in about six seconds in the event of a capsize. With this unique method, the self-righting problem was overcome.

The new design, which became the 37ft Oakley, had many advantages: the weight of the boat was between nine and eleven tons, eminently suitable for handling ashore and carriage launching over a beach, yet the water ballast taken on once afloat provided good sea-keeping qualities and a solid working platform. Most of the boats

Self-righting trial of the prototype 37ft Oakley ON.942 at Littlehampton on 3 June 1958. She had been built at Littlehampton by William Osborne and the trial proved that the new design's water ballast transfer system worked in practice.

On 15 September 1982 the 37ft Oakley from Sheringham, *Manchester Unity of Oddfellows*, proves her self-righting ability at Lowestoft after overhaul and refit at Fletcher's boatyard. (*Lowestoft Journal*, by courtesy of Paul Russell)

that entered service were operated from stations where carriage launching was employed. The self-flooding and emptying water ballast tank, fitted into the bottom, added over a ton of ballast in a position within the hull where it would be of most benefit whilst the boat was afloat. The tank, located beneath the engines, filled automatically in about twenty seconds when the boat entered the water.

Only once has the self-righting capability of the design been called into action on a service launch. Serving at Kilmore Quay in Ireland, *Lady Murphy* (ON.997), the last of the Oakley class to be built, was capsized on 24 December 1977. She was launched in the early hours of the morning following a reported sighting of distress flares off Bannow Bay. After searching without result, the lifeboat was heading back to her station where conditions had worsened. At about 4.30 a.m., about a mile south-south-west of Forlorn Point, the lifeboat was hit by a very high breaking sea which capsized her to port. Acting Second Coxswain Joseph Maddock was thrown overboard. After the boat had righted herself, Acting Mechanic John Devereux started the engines without any difficulty, and the lifeboat was brought alongside the Second Coxswain, who was safely recovered. Part of the lifeboat's windscreen had been shattered and the mast broken during the capsize. As Coxswain Thomas Walsh headed for harbour, a second exceptionally heavy breaking sea hit the lifeboat on her port beam, capsizing her again, this time to starboard. She again righted and the engines were restarted, but this time four crew members had been washed overboard. Three were soon recovered, but the fourth, Finton Sinnott, was not found despite a thorough search involving the Rosslare Harbour lifeboat. Although Acting Second

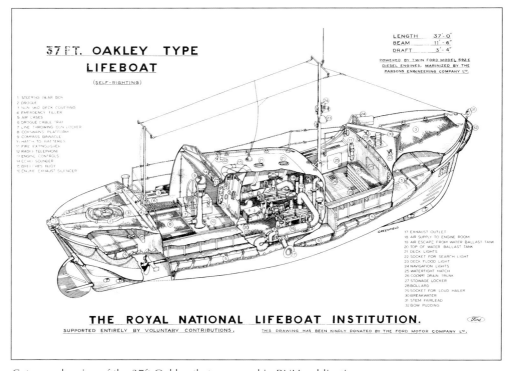

Cutaway drawing of the 37ft Oakley that appeared in RNLI publications.

The prototype 37ft Oakley, *J.G. Graves of Sheffield* at Scarborough in her early days at the station. (Scarborough & District Newspapers, courtesy of RNLI)

Coxswain Joseph Maddock and Acting Assistant Mechanic Dermot Cullerton were injured during the capsize and one life had tragically been lost, the self-righting system undoubtedly saved the rest of the crew.

On several occasions the Oakley's self-righting system was crucial in recovery of the boats after they had suffered a 'knock-down' but had not gone through a complete 360 degree rotation. One of these knock-downs occurred to *The Will and Fanny Kirby* (ON.972) in January 1984 when she was stationed at Flamborough. She was launched from the North Landing at Flamborough in rapidly deteriorating weather conditions to escort three local fishing cobles and, assisted by another Oakley, *Amelia* (ON.979), from Scarborough, went as far north as Whitby. Then she returned south, making for the safety of Scarborough harbour as it was considered too dangerous in the gale force winds to recover her at Flamborough. While off Scarborough, she was caught by a big sea which knocked her down and heeled her over to an angle of approximately 120 degrees, but she came upright thanks to the internal transfer of her water ballast (see entry for ON.979 for further details).

Although the system of self-righting was the most revolutionary aspect of the new design, it also incorporated other technical advances not seen on lifeboats hitherto. Tank tests of a model, held at Cowes on the Isle of Wight, showed that in addition to the self-righting qualities, the hull also had greater initial stability than the non-self-righting 35ft 6in Liverpool class boats then in service which the 37ft Oakley

Lady Murphy returning to Kilmore Quay after she had been capsized on service on 24 December 1977. Although she righted successfully, as she was designed to do, one of the lifeboatmen on board, Finton Sinnott, was lost. (Kilmore Quay Lifeboat Station)

replaced. Stability had been improved by incorporating side casings, the tops of which were formed by a deck at gunwale height. The sea-keeping abilities of the new design were also significantly better: it was less vulnerable to capsize, less susceptible to swamping and kept much better course in confused seas than the Liverpool boat. Although the basic layout, hull shape and construction of the Oakley was similar to that of all previous lifeboat designs, the engine casing was large enough to divide the boat into two cockpits, thereby reducing the area of deck liable to swamping. The relief of any deck water was arranged through tubes from the deck, discharging through the bottom of the boat via pivoted non-return flaps fitted just below deck level.

Some notable developments were incorporated in the machinery installations in the boat. These included capsize cut-off valves in the engine room ventilation system, removable independent fuel tanks in separate watertight compartments and waterproofed exhaust and silencers. In the event of the boat capsizing, provision was made to ensure it could continue to operate: a mechanism to stop the engines was fitted, and non-return valves prevented loss from the water, fuel and oil systems. But despite the technological advances incorporated into the hull, Oakley's new design had little in the way of shelter for the crew. The boats were essentially open with minimal protection for lifeboatmen or survivors apart from the small canopy covering the engine controls. This was one of the few features shared with the previous generation of Liverpool and self-righting motor types.

Because of their hull shape, the 37ft Oakleys were no faster than the lifeboats they replaced. Their speed, however, should be seen in its historical context: in the 1950s

The Will and Fanny Kirby returning to North Landing, Flamborough, in April 1993. This Oakley was put to the test in extreme conditions in January 1984, and was almost capsized while on service. (Richard Martin)

The second Oakley to enter service, *Manchester Unity of Oddfellows*, leaving Gorleston harbour in July 1961 on her way to Sheringham, where she was stationed for almost thirty years. (Eastern Counties Newspapers, by courtesy of Paul Russell)

Two dramatic photographs showing *Charles Fred Grantham. Above:* Launching on service at 11.00 p.m. on 19 May 1965. *Below:* Returning and beaching in heavy seas twelve hours later after towing in a yacht. (Jeff Morris)

The Will and Fanny Kirby on display at the Royal Show, Stoneleigh, in July 1965, promoting the RNLI before going on station at Seaham Harbour in Co. Durham. (Jeff Morris)

speed was not deemed to be as important as self-righting, and so the Oakleys had relatively modest power units compared to the 'fast' lifeboats introduced from the 1960s onwards. The first five Oakleys, completed between 1958 and 1963, were fitted with twin Perkins P4M four-cylinder diesel engines, each developing 43bhp at 2,000rpm with 2:1 reduction gears. A maximum speed of approximately eight knots was achieved, at which rate the engines consumed over four gallons of fuel an hour. Two rectangular thirty-eight gallon capacity aluminium fuel tanks were installed in a common watertight compartment forward of the engine room, giving the boats a radius of action of sixty-eight nautical miles. The remaining boats of the class were fitted with slightly more powerful Ford Parsons Porbeagle four-cylinder diesel engines which developed 52bhp, and a slightly greater fuel capacity. The ninety-six gallons carried gave the boats a range of eighty-seven nautical miles. This engine was also subsequently fitted into two of the earlier boats in place of the original Perkins engines (see Table 2). Those boats fitted with the 52hp Porbeagle diesels had a marginally better performance than the earlier boats powered by Perkins diesels, reaching a maximum speed of a little over 8 knots.

The exhaust was taken from the fore end of each engine, outboard to a water-cooled silencer installed fore and aft against the engine room wing bulkheads, and discharged through the boat's side approximately amidships on the water line. A pendulum-actuated exhaust capsizing valve was fitted to prevent water getting back into the engine in the event of a capsize. Aluminium was used extensively in the construction of the double bottom, bulkheads and engine canopy, which helped to reduce the weight of the total machinery installation. The use of aluminium alloy fuel tanks and piping, however, did not prove satisfactory and these were eventually replaced by stainless steel tanks and copper pipework.

Lilly Wainwright on the promenade at Llandudno together with the Fowler launching tractor. When built, the 37ft Oakleys had a grey engine casing and open aft cockpit. (From a postcard supplied by Mark Roberts)

Table 2: Comparative Performance of 37ft Oakleys 37-01 to 37-13

	Engine Details			Full Speed			Cruising Speed		
Op No.	Engine	BHP	RPM	Revs	Knots	Radius★	Revs	Knots	Radius
37-01	Perkins P4M	43	2000	1004	8.09	73	768	7.0	115
37-02	Perkins P4M	43	2000	995	7.96	70	779	7.0	109
37-03	Perkins P4M	43	2000	998	8.00	70.5	775	7.0	109
37-04	Perkins P4M	43	2000	1001	8.03	66	770	7.0	122
37-05	Perkins P4M	43	2000	1005	8.01	68	770	7.0	120
37-06	Parsons Porbeagle	52	2000	1004	8.1	91	783	7.0	139
37-07	Parsons Porbeagle	52	2000	1005	8.19	86.5	767	7.0	149
37-08	Parsons Porbeagle	52	2000	1001	8.24	85	730	7.0	161
37-09	Parsons Porbeagle	52	2000	1000	8.18	88	744	7.0	170
37-10	Parsons Porbeagle	52	2000	1003	8.21	87	750	7.0	160
37-11	Parsons Porbeagle	52	2000	1004	8.19	80	750	7.0	146
37-12	Parsons Porbeagle	52	2000	1003	8.13	87	760	7.0	166
37-13	Parsons Porbeagle	52	2000	1007	8.16	86.5	753	7.0	149.5

★ Nautical miles

Source: *RNLI, Life-boats and Tractors (Built and Building) and Station Machinery Equipment* (1965)

Once built, the prototype 37ft Oakley underwent extensive trials to prove her capabilities. The first phase of these trials was completed at Littlehampton in June 1958 when she was capsized by crane, an event filmed and shown on the BBC television news. A copy of the film was taken by British Movietone News and shown in cinema newsreels around the country. The second phase of the trials began on 7 June 1958 when the new lifeboat sailed from Littlehampton on an extended sea passage which took her as far north as Dunbar in the Firth of Forth. She was at sea every day and arrived back at Littlehampton on 23 June. Altogether she covered 986 miles during this time and averaged 8.12 knots. Her twin Perkins engines performed reliably and only two or three items of the machinery installation suffered slight defects which were easily rectified.

During this coastal trial, crew and officials from sixteen lifeboat stations had the opportunity of going afloat in the new boat. These stations were Anstruther, Bridlington, Boulmer, Eyemouth, Filey, Flamborough, Hastings, Newbiggin, North Sunderland, Redcar, Runswick, St Abbs, Scarborough, Sheringham, Skegness and Wells, all of which had 35ft 6in lifeboats of either the Liverpool or motor self-righting type. The crews expressed their approval of the new design, regarding the new boat as a considerable improvement on existing types. She was used for a series of launch and recovery trials on the beach at Scarborough using two types of tractor, only one of which, the larger Fowler tractor, had sufficient power to pull the boat across the beach.

Although the majority of 37ft Oakleys were placed at stations where they were carriage launched, a few also served at slipway stations. *Valentine Wyndham-Quin*, seen launching at the end of her naming ceremony, served at Clacton-on-Sea, where she was launched down the slipway built alongside the pier. (Jeff Morris)

In October 1958, the prototype Oakley lifeboat, named *J.G. Graves of Sheffield* (ON.942), entered service at Scarborough. Her first service, and also the first by a 37ft Oakley lifeboat, was performed on 5 December 1958, when she went to the aid of the fishing coble *Rosemary*. During 1959 it was clear that she was more than suitable for the conditions at Scarborough. In the December 1959 edition of *The Lifeboat* it was reported that the prototype had 'fulfilled the demands made upon her to the satisfaction of all'. The success of the boat in operational conditions during 1959 enabled the RNLI to take the decision to build more of the class, and the Institution's Annual Report for 1960 stated that as the prototype 37ft Oakley 'has been found fully satisfactory, two more lifeboats of this type are now under construc-tion'. In 1963 the new design was shown to delegates from around the world at the International Lifeboat Conference held in Edinburgh.

The Royal Thames is recovered on the beach following her arrival at Runswick in September 1970. She served here from 1970 to 1978. (David Phillipson)

One of the last Oakleys to be built, *Vincent Nesfield*, at Eastbourne for her naming ceremony on 9 April 1969. This lifeboat was the first to be built specifically for service in the RNLI's Reserve (later Relief) Fleet. (Jeff Morris)

The 37ft Oakley from St Ives, *Frank Penfold Marshall*, calling at Wells-next-the-Sea in Norfolk on 9 June 1976. She had just been fitted with radar, the first 37ft Oakley so equipped, and was on a tour of lifeboat stations demonstrating it when she called at Wells. (*Eastern Daily Press*, by courtesy of Paul Russell)

Table 3: Technical Details of 37ft Oakley ON.980

Hull	Two thicknesses of African mahogany diagonally laid, separated by a layer of calico; outer skin 0.375in thick, inner skin 0.25in thick
Main deck	Double skin mahogany, upper 0.3125in thick, lower 0.25in thick
Length	37ft
Beam	11ft 6in
Displacement	12.45 tons (loaded with crew and gear)
Keel	Iron, 7.5in deep by 5.125in wide, weight 1.154 tons
Bilge keels	Length 17ft, spread 5ft, height above main keel 5.5ft
Watertight compartments	11
Air cases	219
Range of stability	180 degrees
Relieving trunks	14, size 7.5in by 7.5in
Water ballast	9.12 tons
Carrying capacity	Crew plus 65 in fine weather, 35 in rough weather
Engines	Twin, four-cylinder, Ford Porbeagle diesels, developing 52bhp at 2,000rpm
Cooling system	Closed fresh water, heat exchangers cooled by induction from the sea
Propellers	Twin, 23in diameter by 15in pitch running in tunnels, with a hatch from the deck over each, 1,007rpm full speed, 753rpm cruising speed
Weight of machinery	2.2 tons (including electrical gear)
Fuel capacity	88 gallons
Fuel consumption	4.56gph at full speed, 2.24gph cruising
Speed	8.16 knots maximum, 7 knots cruising
Radius of action	77.5 miles at full speed, 136.5 cruising speed

Source: Ralph Fawcett, *The Bridlington Lifeboats* (1985), pp.69-70.

Sir James Knott launching at Redcar on exercise in the mid-1970s. (David Phillipson)

Between 1957 and 1971, a total of twenty-six 37ft Oakley class lifeboats were built, and most remained in service until the late 1980s. The twenty-sixth and last of the class entered service in 1971, at Kilmore Quay, more than a decade after the prototype was built. In 1993, the last Oakley in service was withdrawn, from Newcastle (Down). The boats had an average service life of just over twenty-six years making their longevity, in terms of British lifeboats, remarkably good. The majority served throughout the 1970s and 1980s and mostly operated from stations which practised carriage launching. At Clacton-on-Sea, Kirkcudbright, Port Erin, Seaham harbour, Weston-super-Mare, Flamborough, Swanage (relief only) and Sennen Cove (relief only), Oakleys were slipway launched.

During their often lengthy service careers, a number of alterations and modifications were carried out to the 37ft Oakleys. When built, many had a white-painted engine casing, but all were subsequently repainted with the RNLI's standard orange and blue livery. Some of the boats were re-engined, and radar was installed during the 1970s by which time a small enough radar scanner had been developed to enable one to be fitted to the boats on a specially-designed mast. The need to manhandle this mast, in order to fold it down so the boats would fit into boathouses, limited the size of scanner that was practical. The first Oakley to be fitted with radar was *Frank Penfold Marshall* (ON.992), which successfully underwent a self-righting trial with the scanner fitted in May 1976. The radar was fitted on a tripod mast at the forward end of the engine casing, designed to hinge forward into the survivor cockpit. The second Oakley to have radar installed was the Clacton-on-Sea boat *Valentine Wyndham-Quin* (ON.985). Not only was radar fitted to all Oakleys in the late 1970s, but the communication equipment was updated to keep in line with the latest technology.

Although originally open boats with little crew protection apart from a small windscreen, in 1982 it was decided to improve the level of crew protection but, as boathouse height was a prime consideration for carriage-launched boats, no fixed structure could be added above the existing casing top. A folding wheelhouse was therefore designed and fitted to a trial boat, which proved an instant success, resulting in enclosed fixed wheelhouses being fitted to all the Oakleys between 1982 and 1986. This was perhaps the most visibly noticeable addition to the boats.

The water ballast tank that gave the 37ft Oakley its stability in the water and enabled it to be self-righting in the event of a capsize proved somewhat problematic in the long-term. The aluminium alloy construction of the inner bottom, which on entry into the water was filled with salt water, acted like a giant battery on the wooden hull and over time caused the hull to deteriorate. During the mid-1980s several of the Oakleys in service suffered serious problems of hull deterioration and, as a result, many had to be virtually rebuilt, something of an expensive and time-consuming process.

The Doctors being rebuilt at Buckie Boatyard after suffering from serious hull deterioration. (Tony Denton)

Lloyds II entering Lowestoft after leaving Sheringham on 18 April 1992. The boat was, at this time, in the twilight of her career and shows the modifications made to the Oakleys during their service careers which included a radar mast and an enclosed cockpit. (Paul Russell)

Although improvements were made to the original design and incorporated into the boats that had been built, in 1972 it was decided to re-design the Oakley. The object was to accommodate radar in a boat that was the smallest in service with the RNLI, and also provide enclosed accommodation for the crew. The new design was similar in many aspects to the Oakley and the hull shape was almost identical, though the hull itself was lengthened at the bow by 6in. The most noticeable difference between the Oakley and Rother was the long, almost full-length water-tight casing which stretched from the fore buoyancy chamber to the aft end of the engine room. The enclosed fore cabin, with access through the engine room and an escape hatch in the roof provided, for the first time in a small boat, a watertight survivor cabin.

Most important of all, a new method of self-righting was employed. To build a cabin motor lifeboat which is both inherently stable with good sea-keeping abilities and self-righting, one of three techniques can be employed. The first is similar to that of the early self-righting lifeboats: a substantial watertight wheelhouse with closed watertight doors, roughly equivalent to the high end-boxes of the first self-righters, which renders the hull unstable in the upturned position, and thus brings it upright; this system has been used by the RNLI for all new offshore lifeboat designs since the 1970s. The second is the water ballast transfer system, described above. And the third is the air-bag, which provides a lifeboat with a once-only righting capacity. This was introduced in 1972, fitted retrospectively to many offshore lifeboats, and is used today on Atlantic rigid-inflatable inshore lifeboats.

While the 37ft Oakley design employed the water ballast transfer system, this was abandoned in the modified design in favour of a watertight superstructure large enough to make the boat inherently unstable when capsized. A hollow wheelhouse roof was also incorporated into the design to aid self-righting. This almost fully enclosed the cockpit which was open only at the rear, although this was eventually closed with a clear plastic screen in most of the boats. The space originally given over to the water ballast tank in the Oakleys was taken up by a double-bottom void

The first Rother to be built, *Osman Gabriel*, moored at William Osborne, Littlehampton, in September 1972 during her final fitting out and completion. (Jeff Morris)

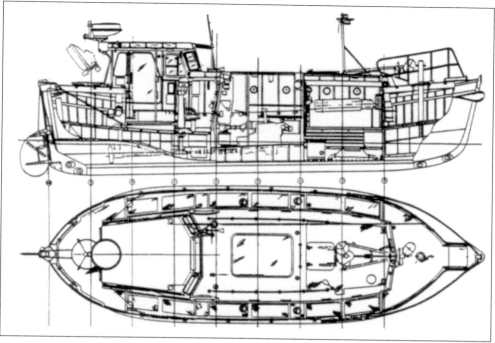

Cutaway drawing of 37ft 6in Rother class lifeboat from *The Lifeboat*, Vol. XLIV, No.457, Autumn 1976, p.203.

ensuring that the engine room would not be flooded if the hull was holed. The radar scanner was fitted at the aft end of the wheelhouse roof and hinged to swing down into a stowed position beneath the roofline to conform to the restricted headroom of existing boathouses at stations where they served.

The new design was given the class name Rother after a tributary of the River Arun which flows through Littlehampton where the first of the class was built. This first Rother successfully completed her self-righting trial on 9 September 1972 watched by Major Osman Gabriel, of Hove, who had generously funded the boat. Named *Osman Gabriel* (ON.998), she was displayed at the Earl's Court Boat Show in London in January 1973, and entered service at Port Erin in July 1973. During the 1970s the RNLI placed orders for the construction of further Rothers and in total fourteen of the class were built between 1972 and 1982.

Although the Rother was in theory a new design when it entered service in the 1970s, it was in fact based on old technology. The displacement hull was similar to late nineteenth-century lifeboats and, fitted with relatively small engines, its slow speed was a major drawback at a time when faster lifeboats were becoming the norm. By the end of the 1980s when a new, 17 knot lifeboat suitable for carriage launching was introduced, some Rothers were replaced having been operational for little more than a decade. The replacement, which became known as the 12m Mersey, was a significant advance in lifeboat technology. The Mersey was designed to be light enough for carriage launching, while incorporating a fully enclosed wheelhouse offering complete crew protection, a self-righting capability and most significantly a

The tenth 37ft 6in Rother lifeboat to be built, *Shoreline*, seen off Cromer in 1979 while on passage to her station at Blyth in Northumberland. *(Studio G Photography, by courtesy of Paul Russell)*

James Cable, the last Rother to be built, was stationed at Aldeburgh for little more than a decade. This photograph shows her approaching the beach at Aldeburgh. She was completed in 1982 and was the last wooden-hulled lifeboat to be built for service with the RNLI. (Jeff Morris)

speed twice that of the Oakley and Rother. The design was developed during the mid-1980s and by 1987 a prototype had been built and was undergoing trials at various stations around the coast where carriage launching was employed. The first boats built to the new design were constructed from aluminium, while a second series was constructed using fibre-reinforced composite, an advanced material that combined strength with relative light weight. Following the success of the production prototypes and their entry into service at Bridlington and Hastings in place of Oakleys, a full building programme of new Merseys was soon underway.

As more Merseys were completed during the early 1990s, Oakleys and Rothers were gradually taken out of service. In 1986, during the development of the Mersey, the RNLI set a target date of 1993 when it was intended to have 'fast' lifeboats operating from every lifeboat station equipped with an all-weather lifeboat. The rapid replacement of the 37ft lifeboats was central to meeting this target and in November 1993 the last Rother to be taken out of service, *James Cable* (ON.1068), was replaced by the 12m Mersey *Freddie Cooper* (ON.1193) at Aldeburgh. This boat was also the last of the traditional double-ended lifeboats in service, and when she left the lifeboat service she also ended a tradition of lifeboat design that had lasted for more than two centuries. The era of displacement-hulled lifeboats, whose origins could be traced back to the origins of the lifeboat itself, was at an end.

William Henry and Mary King off the harbour at Bridlington with the prototype 12m Mersey (ON.1125) during trials of the latter in February 1988. (Paul Russell)

12m Mersey *Inchcape* (ON.1194) on exercise off Arbroath in August 2002. The Mersey replaced many Oakleys and Rothers during the early 1990s. (Nicholas Leach)

James Ball Ritchie with her successor, 12m Mersey *Ann and James Ritchie* (ON.1171), off Ramsey, Isle of Man, on 27 July 1991. The arrival of a new lifeboat is a major event in the history of any lifeboat station. (Tony Denton)

J.G. Graves of Sheffield on relief duty at Margate, seen outside the lifeboat house. After being stationed at Scarborough, the prototype 37ft Oakley served for many years as a Relief lifeboat. (Paul Russell)

Manchester Unity of Oddfellows returning to the beach at Sheringham on 4 September 1976 with the crew of two rescued from the barge *Focena*. The difficulties of recovering a lifeboat on an open beach in heavy surf are clearly shown in this dramatic photograph. (Eastern Counties Newspapers, by courtesy of Paul Russell)

Calouste Gulbenkian on the slipway at Weston-super-Mare. She was the last all-weather lifeboat to operate from this slipway. (From a postcard supplied by a Shoreline member)

Calouste Gulbenkian on passage through Ramsgate. She served for much of her RNLI career in the Relief Fleet. This photograph shows how the Oakleys looked during the final years of their service, with enclosed wheelhouse and radar mast. (Phil Weeks)

Robert and Dorothy Hardcastle being recovered at Filey in August 1983. (Paul Russell)

The Will and Fanny Kirby being recovered at North Landing, Flamborough. This photograph shows the steepness of the slipway at North Landing, and the effort required to recover the Oakley. (Richard Martin)

Jane Hay in the harbour at Newcastle (Co. Down). Originally built for St Abbs, this Oakley served at Newcastle for more than a decade. (R. McLaughlin)

The Royal Thames launching for Flag Day at Caister in August 1964. She was later stationed at Runswick and Pwllheli. (Jeff Morris)

Amelia beaching at Scarborough in September 1991, to be recovered across the beach by the Talus MB-H launching tractor. *Amelia* was the second 37ft Oakley to be stationed at Scarborough, as she replaced the prototype in 1978. (Paul Russell)

William Henry and Mary King beaching at Cromer in 1964. She served as the No.2 lifeboat at Cromer from 1964 until 1967, and was then stationed at Bridlington for more than twenty years. (Eastern Counties Newspapers, by courtesy of Paul Russell)

Mary Pullman at sea off Kirkcudbright in July 1988. *Mary Pullman* was one of only three Oakleys to serve at stations in Scotland. (Tony Denton)

Ernest Tom Neathercoat on exercise off the Norfolk coast while stationed at Wells-next-the-Sea. After serving this Norfolk station for a quarter of a century, she later returned to be displayed there. (Paul Russell)

Recovery of *Ernest Tom Neathercoat* at Seahouses harbour while on temporary station duty at the North Sunderland station in the early 1990s. (Richard Martin)

Mary Joicey being lifted onto a road trailer to be taken away from Redcar on 26 March 1986. She was the last all-weather lifeboat to serve at the station, having stood in as a relief lifeboat for *Sir James Knott*. After the withdrawal of *Mary Joicey*, Redcar station was served by an Atlantic 21 and D class inflatable. (David Phillipson)

Har-Lil on the promenade outside the lifeboat house at Rhyl. She served this station for more than twenty years. (From a postcard supplied by Mark Roberts)

Vincent Nesfield being recovered at Hoylake in May 1982. This Oakley lifeboat served at many stations during her service career, relieving both Oakleys and Rothers that were taken away for overhaul and routine maintenance. (Tony Denton)

Manchester Unity of Oddfellows and relief lifeboat *Vincent Nesfield* outside the lifeboat house at Sheringham on 8 November 1976 during a routine changeover with the former to go for overhaul. (Eastern Counties Newspapers, courtesy of Paul Russell)

Birds Eye at Dickie's Boat Yard, Bangor, on 13 November 1984 following a major refit during which the boat was fitted with an enclosed aft cockpit. (Tony Denton)

Diana White alongside the slipway at Sennen Cove prior to recovery. The lifeboat was launched down one slipway and recovered bow-first up another, a system unique to Sennen Cove. (Peter Puddiphatt)

Recovery of *Harold Salvesen* on the beach at Rhyl in June 1992 after she had been launched to escort her replacement, 12m Mersey *Lil Cunningham* (ON.1183), into the harbour. After a period of crew training, the new Mersey was officially placed on station on 23 June 1992 and *Harold Salvesen* was withdrawn. (Nicholas Leach)

Mary Gabriel on the beach at Hoylake on 12 October 1990. The lifeboat house can be seen in the background to the right. (Nicholas Leach)

Above and below: The Hampshire Rose served at Walmer from 1975 to 1990. In 1990 she was replaced by an Atlantic 21 rigid-inflatable inshore lifeboat, so her withdrawal meant the end of the offshore lifeboat era at Walmer. These two photographs show the events of 6 May 1990 when she left Walmer. After a service of thanksgiving conducted on the beach by the Vicar of Walmer, the Revd Bruce Hawkins, Chaplain to the Walmer station, *The Hampshire Rose* was launched for the last time in front of a crowd of several thousand people with the lifeboats from Dover and Ramsgate in attendance. (Paul Russell)

Alice Upjohn being recovered on the beach at Dungeness on 16 August 1992. (Paul Russell)

Duke of Kent being recovered at Eastbourne in August 1991. This photograph shows the procedure undertaken to recover the boat: she was hauled out of the water by a winch, over skids laid on the beach, onto a turntable on which she was turned through 90 degrees, then pulled into the boathouse stern first. (Nicholas Leach)

Princess of Wales at Barmouth on 25 November 1982 prior to her naming and dedication ceremony. (Tony Denton)

The once-familiar sight of *James Cable*, the last Rother to be built, on the cradle at the head of the beach at Aldeburgh. (Nicholas Leach)

On the beach at Filey: 37ft Oakley *Robert and Dorothy Hardcastle* (left) alongside her replacement *Keep Fit Association* (ON.1170), a 12m Mersey class that was almost twice as fast, with the Filey lifeboat crew, shore helpers and Talus launching tractor (to right). (Graham Taylor)

Mary Gabriel with her successor, 12m Mersey *Lady of Hilbre* (ON.1163), on the beach at Hoylake, just outside the lifeboat house after the latter had arrived on station for the first time in October 1990. (Nicholas Leach)

Launching trials at Aldeburgh, May 1990: Rother *James Cable* on the cradle at the top of the beach, with relief 12m Mersey *Lifetime Care* (ON.1148) on the launching carriage. The trials with the Mersey determined that it was possible to launch the Mersey from a carriage on Aldeburgh's shingle beach and thus do away with the slipway, cradle and skids used hitherto. The Mersey's semi-planing hull gave the boat a speed of 16 knots, almost twice that of the Rother. (Paul Russell)

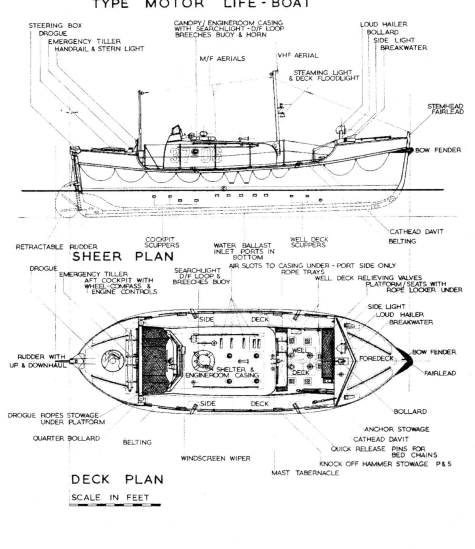

37 FT 'OAKLEY' TWIN SCREW SELF-RIGHTING TYPE MOTOR LIFE-BOAT

STEERING BOX
DROGUE
EMERGENCY TILLER
HANDRAIL & STERN LIGHT

CANOPY/ENGINEROOM CASING WITH SEARCHLIGHT - D/F LOOP BREECHES BUOY & HORN

M/F AERIALS

VHF AERIAL

STEAMING LIGHT & DECK FLOODLIGHT

LOUD HAILER
BOLLARD
SIDE LIGHT
BREAKWATER

STEMHEAD FAIRLEAD

BOW FENDER

CATHEAD DAVIT
BELTING

RETRACTABLE RUDDER

COCKPIT SCUPPERS

WATER BALLAST INLET PORTS IN BOTTOM

WELL DECK SCUPPERS

SHEER PLAN

DROGUE
EMERGENCY TILLER
AFT COCKPIT WITH
WHEEL-COMPASS &
ENGINE CONTROLS

SEARCHLIGHT
D/F LOOP &
BREECHES BUOY

AIR SLOTS TO CASING UNDER - PORT SIDE ONLY
ROPE TRAYS

WELL DECK RELIEVING VALVES
PLATFORM/SEATS WITH
ROPE LOCKER UNDER

SIDE LIGHT
LOUD HAILER
BREAKWATER

RUDDER WITH
UP & DOWNHAUL

SIDE   DECK

WELL
DECK

SHELTER &
ENGINEROOM CASING

WELL
DECK

FOREDECK

SIDE   DECK

BOW FENDER

FAIRLEAD

BOLLARD

DROGUE ROPES STOWAGE
UNDER PLATFORM

QUARTER BOLLARD

BELTING

WINDSCREEN WIPER

MAST TABERNACLE

ANCHOR STOWAGE
CATHEAD DAVIT
QUICK RELEASE PINS FOR
BED CHAINS
KNOCK OFF HAMMER STOWAGE P & S

DECK PLAN

SCALE IN FEET

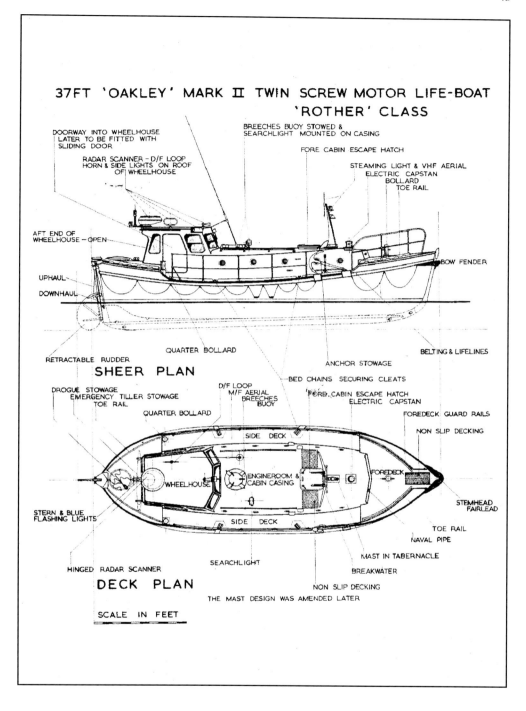

37FT 'OAKLEY' MARK II TWIN SCREW MOTOR LIFE-BOAT 'ROTHER' CLASS

DOORWAY INTO WHEELHOUSE
LATER TO BE FITTED WITH
SLIDING DOOR

RADAR SCANNER – D/F LOOP
HORN & SIDE LIGHTS ON ROOF
OF WHEELHOUSE

BREECHES BUOY STOWED &
SEARCHLIGHT MOUNTED ON CASING

FORE CABIN ESCAPE HATCH

STEAMING LIGHT & VHF AERIAL
ELECTRIC CAPSTAN
BOLLARD
TOE RAIL

AFT END OF
WHEELHOUSE – OPEN

BOW FENDER

UPHAUL

DOWNHAUL

QUARTER BOLLARD

BELTING & LIFELINES

RETRACTABLE RUDDER

ANCHOR STOWAGE

SHEER PLAN

BED CHAINS SECURING CLEATS

DROGUE STOWAGE
EMERGENCY TILLER STOWAGE
TOE RAIL

D/F LOOP
M/F AERIAL
BREECHES
BUOY

FORE CABIN ESCAPE HATCH
ELECTRIC CAPSTAN

QUARTER BOLLARD

FOREDECK GUARD RAILS

NON SLIP DECKING

SIDE DECK

WHEELHOUSE

ENGINEROOM &
CABIN CASING

FOREDECK

STEMHEAD
FAIRLEAD

STERN & BLUE
FLASHING LIGHTS

SIDE DECK

TOE RAIL

NAVAL PIPE

MAST IN TABERNACLE

HINGED RADAR SCANNER

SEARCHLIGHT

BREAKWATER

NON SLIP DECKING

DECK PLAN

THE MAST DESIGN WAS AMENDED LATER

SCALE IN FEET

2

Lifeboats

Abbreviations used in the lists

Alts	alterations	I	Inspection	sl	station lifeboat
CT	Crew training	M	Maintenance	SRT	Self-righting trials
Dis	display	ON	Official Number	Std	Stored
ER	Emergency Relief	Ovh	Overhaul	T	Trials
ET	Evaluation Trials	R	Repairs	TSD	Temporary Station
H	Hull	RE	Re-engined		Duty
HC	Hull clean	rlvd	relieved by	uc	Under construction
HR	Hull rebuilt,	rlvg	relieving	wh	Wheelhouse
	replanked or	S	Survey	7/2	launches/lives saved
	repaired	S&R	Survey and Repairs		

A dramatic photograph of *The Will and Fanny Kirby* launching from North Landing, Flamborough, in 1993. (Paul Arro)

Oakleys

J.G. Graves of Sheffield

Official Number	942
Operational Number	37-01
Year built	1957
Builder	William Osborne, Littlehampton
Yard No.	WO 942
Cost	£26,700
Donor	Gift of the J.G. Graves Charitable Trust.
Named	11 June 1959 at Scarborough, by Lady Georgina Starkey.

Stations

Scarborough	Oct. 1958 – Nov. 1978	105/9
Relief	Nov. 1978 – Sept. 1988	31/9
Clogher Head	Sept. 1988 – Mar. 1991	9/3
Newcastle	Aug. 1992 – Sept. 1993	16/0

Movements

1.10.1958 – 28.5.1962	Scarborough (sl)
28.5.1962 – 29.6.1962	Harrisons Bt Yd, Amble (rlvd by ON.797)
29.6.1962 – 24.5.1965	Scarborough (sl)
24.5.1965 – 30.11.1965	Harrisons Bt Yd, Amble (rlvd by ON.979)
30.11.1965 – 4.10.1970	Scarborough (sl)
4.10.1970 – 13.4.1971	Harrisons Bt Yd, Amble (rlvd by ON.961)
13.4.1971 – 8.11.1978	Scarborough (sl)
8.11.1978 – 3.2.1979	Coastal Marine, Eyemouth
3.2.1979 – 19.5.1979	Anstruther (rlvd ON.983)
19.5.1979 – 20.5.1979	Passage to Redcar
20.5.1979 – 12.6.1979	Redcar (rlvd ON.975)
12.6.1979 – 14.6.1979	Passage to Thorne
14.6.1979 – 15.9.1979	Staniland's Bt Yd, Thorne (S)
15.9.1979 – 15.10.1979	Skegness (rlvd ON.977)
15.10.1979 – 31.10.1979	Staniland's Bt Yd, Thorne (T)
31.10.1979 – 9.11.1979	Passage (assisting ON.1066 on trials at Rye)
9.11.1979 – 16.11.1979	Staniland's Bt Yd, Thorne (ER)
17.11.1979 – 24.11.1979	Passage (at Bridlington for launching trials at Flamborough)
24.11.1979 – 22.3.1980	Staniland's Bt Yd, Thorne (T)
22.3.1980 – 23.3.1980	Passage to Scarborough
23.3.1980 – 17.4.1980	Scarborough (rlvd ON.979)

J.G. Graves of Sheffield entering Whitby harbour for the naming ceremony of *The White Rose of Yorkshire*. (Jeff Morris)

17.4.1980 – 18.4.1980	Passage to Thorne
18.4.1980 – 10.8.1982	Staniland's Bt Yd, Thorne (ER, std)
10.8.1981 – 16.8.1981	Displayed at the Canal Festival, Leeds (publicity boat)
16.8.1980 – 29.5.1982	Staniland's Bt Yd, Thorne (ER, std)
29.5.1982 – 4.6.1982	Passage inland (Canals Tour as part of Nottinghamshire Lifeboat Appeal and for general fundraising to Lincoln and the Trent; 28 April to 12 May from Thorne to Lincoln Marina, via Keadby Lock, Cromwell Lock, Newark Marina and Town Lock, British Waterways Board HQ, Nottingham, BWB Fisheries & Pollution Office, Torksey Lock)
4.6.1982 – 22.12.1982	Staniland's Bt Yd, Thorne (ER, std)
22.12.1982 – 29.12.1982	Passage to Bangor
29.12.1982 – 5.5.1983	Dickie's Bt Yd, Bangor (R, ER)
5.5.1983 – 17.12.1983	Pwllheli (rlvd ON.978)
17.12.1983 – 1.2.1984	Dickie's Bt Yd, Bangor (ER)
1.2.1984 – 11.7.1984	Robson's Bt Yd, South Shields (radar and fixed w/h fitted, std)
11.7.1984 – 17.9.1984	Blyth (std in btho, ER)
17.9.1984 – 18.9.1984	Passage overland to Lymington
18.9.1984 – 19.9.1984	Berthon Bt Co., Lymington
19.9.1984 – 8.3.1985	Swanage (rlvd ON.1023: 8/5)
8.3.1985 – 9.3.1985	RNLI Depot, Poole (for passage)
9.3.1985 – 15.3.1985	Passage to Clogher Head
15.3.1985 – 16.4.1985	Clogher Head (rlvd ON.985: 0/0)
16.4.1985 – 20.4.1985	Arklow (rlvd ON.907)

20.4.1985 – 21.4.1985	Passage to Ilfracombe
21.4.1985 – 2.7.1985	Ilfracombe (rlvd ON.986: 1/0)
2.7.1985 – 4.7.1985	Passage to Ramsey
4.7.1985 – 7.8.1985	Ramsey (rlvd ON.995: 1/0)
7.8.1985 – 8.8.1985	Kirkcudbright (rlvd ON.981: 0/0)
8.8.1985 – 18.10.1985	Rhyl (rlvd ON.993: 2/0)
18.10.1985 – 26.10.1985	Llandudno (rlvd ON.976: 0/0)
26.10.1985 – 6.11.1985	Dickie's Bt Yd, Bangor (I, ER)
6.11.1985 – 7.11.1985	Passage to RNLI Depot (overland)
7.11.1985 – 8.11.1985	RNLI Depot, Poole
8.11.1985 – 9.11.1985	Passage to Margate
9.11.1985 – 7.8.1986	Margate (rlvd ON.1046: 9/4)
7.8.1986 – 12.2.1988	Crescent Marine, Otterham Qy (HR)
12.2.1988 – 13.2.1988	Passage overland to Bangor
13.2.1988 – 18.2.1988	Dickie's Bt Yd, Bangor (ER)
18.2.1988 – 6.9.1988	Hoylake (rlvd ON.1000: 5/0)
6.9.1988 – 9.9.1988	Holyhead Bt Yd, Anglesey (ER)
9.9.1988 – 9.9.1988	Clogher Head (TSD)
9.9.1988 – 10.9.1988	Passage to Kilmore Quay (CT, return to Clogher Head)
10.9.1988 – 29.3.1991	Clogher Head (TSD)
29.3.1991 – 30.3.1991	Passage to Tyrrells Bt Yd
30.3.1991 – 19.10.1991	Tyrrells Bt Yd, Arklow (S)
19.10.1991 – 30.11.1991	Clogher Head (TSD)
30.11.1991 – 2.8.1992	Tyrrells Bt Yd, Arklow (std, replaced at Clogher Hd by ON.978)
1.12.1991 – 2.8.1992	Tyrrells Bt Yd, Arklow (ER)
2.8.1992 – 3.8.1992	Passage to Newcastle
3.8.1992 – 22.9.1993	Newcastle (Down) (rlvd ON.974)
22.9.1993 – 24.9.1993	Newcastle (Down) (rlvd ON.1188)
24.9.1993 – 25.9.1993	Passage to Bangor (via Port St Mary)
25.9.1993 – 11.8.1994	Dickie's Bt Yd, Bangor (std)
11.8.1994 – 12.8.1994	Passage overland to Chatham Historic Dockyard (dis)

Notable Rescues

On 23 November 1969, when stationed at Scarborough, *J.G. Graves of Sheffield* was involved in a remarkable service during which she was taken in among dangerous outcrops of rock. The rescue began shortly after midday when the lifeboat was launched in a strong north-easterly wind and very rough sea to the converted ships' lifeboat *Sheena*, which had capsized in South Bay. The lifeboat reached the casualty within five minutes of being launched, battling through the very rough, heavy seas that were breaking in the bay

On arriving at the scene, the casualty was found to be in a perilous position close inshore in very shallow water. Coxswain William Sheader skilfully manoeuvred the lifeboat through heavy breakers and the lifeboatmen managed to pull one survivor out of the water. He was landed at the harbour, and the lifeboat went out again to find another survivor.

Although the lifeboat was in grave danger, touching the bottom at one point, another man was successfully pulled out of the water. As soon as the lifeboat reached the harbour, he was rushed to hospital but later died. After this outstanding service, the lifeboat then went out again and assisted the cobles *Eileen* and *Faithful*.

For this service, the Silver medal was awarded to Coxswain Sheader; the Thanks on Vellum was accorded to each of the other members of the crew: Second Coxswain Thomas Rowley, Mechanic Allen Rennard, Assistant Mechanic Cecil Bean, Emergency Mechanic Robert Swalwell and crew members Jack Rowley and George Plumber.

J.G. Graves of Sheffield was involved in another medal–winning rescue while stationed at Scarborough. Just before midnight on 29 September 1973 she was launched, with Second Coxswain Thomas Rowley in charge, in a force eight gale and very rough sea after red flares had been sighted off Scarborough Castle. As she searched for the casualty, reported in Cayton Bay, the weather worsened. By the time the casualty was spotted, the wind had reached force ten.

Once on the scene, the lifeboat went round the casualty, the ex-harbour defence motor launch *Eun-Mara-An-Tar*, and Second Coxswain Rowley assessed the situation. The casualty's steering gear had broken and the skipper was preparing to abandon ship. After several attempts to pass a rope, the casualty's crew succeeded in attaching it to their vessel. Once the towline had been successfully connected, a slow passage to Scarborough began. Although the rope parted on three occasions, the motor launch and its crew of four were eventually brought safely into harbour. For this service, the Bronze medal was awarded to Acting Coxswain Rowley and medal certificates presented to the rest of the crew.

Disposal

After a long service career, *J.G. Graves of Sheffield* was taken by road from Dickie's Bt Yd, Bangor, on 12 August 1994 to the Historic Dockyard at Chatham where she was placed on display as part of the National Lifeboat Collection.

———— *Manchester Unity of Oddfellows* ————

Official Number	960
Operational Number	37–02
Year built	1960
Builder	William Osborne, Littlehampton
Yard No.	WO 960
Cost	£28,500
Donor	Gift of Independent Order of Odd Fellows, Manchester Unity Friendly Society.
Named	15 June 1962 by HRH Princess Marina, Duchess of Kent, at Sheringham.

Stations

Sheringham	Jul. 1961 – Oct. 1990	126/74

Manchester Unity of Oddfellows launching from Sheringham during the early years of her service career with her superstructure painted grey. (From a postcard supplied by Mark Roberts)

Movements

1.1.1960 – 20.6.1961	William Osborne, Littlehampton (uc)
20.6.1961 – 21.6.1961	Passage to Lowestoft, via Dover
21.6.1961 – 9.7.1961	Taken overland to the Royal Show, Cambridge (dis)
10.7.1961 – 10.7.1961	Passage to Sheringham
10.7.1961 – 27.4.1981	Sheringham (sl)
27.4.1981 – 29.10.1982	Fletchers Bt Yd, Lowestoft (S, RE: 2x52hp Ford Thornycroft diesels)
6.10.1982 – 29.10.1982	Lowestoft (T)
29.10.1982 – 31.10.1982	Passage to Sheringham (DI aboard)
31.10.1982 – 22.7.1984	Sheringham (sl)
22.7.1984 – 23.7.1984	Passage to Woodbridge
23.7.1984 – 4.8.1984	Whisstocks Bt Yd, Woodbridge (R)
4.8.1984 – 7.12.1985	Sheringham (sl)
7.12.1985 – 8.12.1985	Passage to Otterham Quay
8.12.1985 – 22.10.1986	Crescent Marine, Otterham Quay (S, RH)
22.10.1986 – 24.10.1986	Passage to Sheringham
24.10.1986 – 8.10.1990	Sheringham (sl)
8.10.1990 – 10.10.1990	Passage to Otterham Quay (via Lowestoft and Harwich)
10.10.1990 – 30.4.1991	Crescent Bt Yd, Otterham Quay

Notable Rescue

At 1.15 p.m. on 15 August 1961, The *Manchester Unity of Oddfellows* was launched in a northerly force eight wind and rough seas to the converted ships' lifeboat *Lucy*. She was five miles north-east of Sheringham, taking water on board and her engines were out of action. There were two men, one woman and a boy on board.

Under the command of Coxswain Henry West, the lifeboat reached the casualty. Twice the lifeboat was taken alongside, enabling three lifeboatmen to board the vessel. They found the woman on board unconscious and the two men were too busy at the pumps to attend to her. So the lifeboat went alongside again and she was taken off by the lifeboatmen.

Despite the efforts of those on board, the situation of the *Lucy* was becoming dangerous and she was in danger of capsizing because of the short, steep sea and the amount of free surface water aboard her. Coxswain West then took the lifeboat alongside again and took off another of the casualty's crew. The three members of the lifeboat crew who were still on board the casualty did not have time to jump, but the two boats were washed together and all three men managed to scramble aboard the lifeboat.

The lifeboat's Bowman, A. Scotter, who had been on the casualty, was in danger of being crushed between the two boats, but he managed to pull himself away just in time. The lifeboat then returned to Sheringham where she was beached. A doctor attended to the woman, who had recovered consciousness with the aid of the lifeboat crew. The casualty itself drifted ashore at Salthouse. For this rescue, during which the lifeboat saved four persons, the Thanks on Vellum was accorded to Coxswain West, Second Coxswain R.H. West, Bowman R. Scotter, and Signalman E. Wink.

Recovery of *Manchester Unity of Oddfellows* at Sheringham on 4 August 1984 using a Fowler tractor. (Paul Russell)

Manchester Unity of Oddfellows at sea off Sheringham, with her superstructure painted white and a canvas cover for the aft cockpit. (From a postcard supplied by Mark Roberts)

Disposal

Sold 30 April 1991 for £585.50 to the Sheringham Museum Trust, *Manchester Unity of Oddfellows* was placed on display outside at the Muckleburgh Collection, Weybourne, Norfolk, together with another former Sheringham lifeboat, *J.C. Madge* (ON.536). She was then stored at Aylsham until 1999 when she became part of the Sheringham lifeboat collection.

Calouste Gulbenkian

Official Number	961
Operational Number	37-03
Year built	1961
Builder	J.S. White, Cowes
Yard No.	W 5496
Cost	£34,000
Donor	Gift of the Calouste Gulbenkian Foundation.
Named	22 September 1962 at Weston-super-Mare, by Mrs K.L. Essayan, daughter of the late Calouste Gulbenkian.

Stations

Weston-super-Mare	Mar. 1962 – Apr. 1970	33/6
Relief	April 1970 – Nov. 1991	107/15

Calouste Gulbenkian moored at Gorleston whilst on passage as a reserve lifeboat. (John Markham)

Movements

17.9.1959 – 10.10.1961	J.S. White, Cowes (construction)
3.1961 – 10.1961	Cowes (T)
10.10.1961 – 12.10.1961	J.S. White, Cowes (awaiting passage)
12.10.1961 – 18.10.1961	Passage to Weston-super-Mare
18.10.1961 – 11.11.1961	Weston-super-Mare (sl)
11.11.1961 – 31.12.1961	Blackmore Bt Yd (R, damaged at Weston-super-Mare)
31.12.1961 – 30.4.1970	Weston-super-Mare (sl)
30.4.1970 – 30.9.1970	Appledore Sh Yd (S for Relief Fleet)
30.9.1970 – 4.10.1970	Passage to Scarborough
4.10.1970 – 13.4.1971	Scarborough (rlvd ON.942: 4/0)
13.4.1971 – 23.5.1971	Filey (rlvd ON.966: 2/0)
23.5.1971 – 12.11.1971	Sheringham (rlvd ON.960: 1/2)
13.6.1972 – 15.6.1972	Seaham (rlvd ON.972: 1/0)
3.12.1972 – 5.8.1973	Skegness (rlvd ON.977: 2/0)
5.8.1973 – 13.4.1974	Bridlington (rlvd ON.980: 9/3)
13.4.1974 – 16.4.1974	Passage to Anstruther
16.4.1974 – 8.5.1976	Anstruther (rlvd ON.983: 3/0)
8.5.1976 – 13.11.1976	Clacton-on-Sea (rlvd ON.985: 7/2)
13.11.1976 – 14.11.1976	Passage to Wells
14.11.1976 – 25.9.1977	Wells (rlvd ON.982: 5/0)
29.9.1977 – 16.4.1978	Skegness (rlvd ON.977: 4/0)
19.4.1978 – 25.4.1978	Passage to St Ives
25.4.1978 – 6.5.1979	St Ives (rlvd ON.992: 10/0)
6.5.1979 – 10.5.1979	Passage to Hastings

10.5.1979 – 27.10.1979	Hastings (rlvd ON.973: 5/0)
27.10.1979 – 28.10.1979	Passage to Swanage
28.10.1979 – 18.2.1980	Swanage (rlvd ON.1023: 4/0)
18.2.1980 – 20.2.1980	Passage to Rowhedge
20.2.1980 – 9.8.1980	Brown's Bt Yd, Rowhedge (S)
9.8.1980 – 14.3.1981	Clacton-on-Sea (rlvd ON.985: 6/0)
14.3.1981 – 21.3.1981	Brown's Bt Yd, Rowhedge
21.3.1981 – 24.4.1981	Margate (rlvd ON.1046: 2/0)
24.4.1981 – 26.4.1981	Passage to Sheringham
26.4.1981 – 1.11.1982	Sheringham (rlvd ON.960: 7/0)
1.11.1982 – 2.11.1982	Passage to Rowhedge
2.11.1982 – 4.12.1982	Brown's Bt Yd, Rowhedge (S)
4.12.1982 – 5.12.1982	Passage to Wells
5.12.1982 – 25.7.1983	Wells (rlvd ON.982: 5/0)
25.7.1983 – 22.7.1984	Skegness (rlvd ON.977: 4/0)
22.7.1984 – 5.8.1984	Sheringham (rlvd ON.960: 1/0)
5.8.1984 – 13.8.1984	Fletchers Bt Yd, Lowestoft (I)
13.8.1984 – 14.8.1984	Passage to Hastings
14.8.1984 – 2.4.1985	Hastings (rlvd ON.973: 6/0)
2.4.1985 – 31.8.1985	Cantell's Bt Yd, Newhaven (S)
31.8.1985 – 1.9.1985	Passage to Margate
1.9.1985 – 12.9.1985	Margate (rlvd ON.1046: 0/0)
12.9.1985 – 2.12.1986	Brown's Bt Yd, Rowhedge (S)
2.12.1986 – 3.12.1986	Passage to Wells
3.12.1986 – 23.5.1988	Wells (rlvd ON.982: 4/5)
23.5.1988 – 18.12.1989	Llandudno (rlvd ON.976: 9/3)
18.12.1989 – 19.12.1989	Passage to Bangor
19.12.1989 – 26.1.1990	Dickie's Bt Yd, Bangor (ER, S)
27.1.1990 – 27.1.1991	New Quay (Dyfed) (TSD: 6/0)
27.1.1991 – 28.1.1991	Passage to Pembroke Dock (via Fishguard)
28.1.1991 – 4.2.1991	Marine Port Services, Pembroke Dock (S, I)
4.2.1991 – 30.11.1991	Marine Port Services, Pembroke Dock (ER)

Notable Rescue

One of the most outstanding rescues in which *Calouste Gulbenkian* was involved took place on 20 November 1984, while she was on relief duty at Hastings, when the container ship *Bell Rover*, of Waterford, requested that a sick crewman be taken off. As the case involved drug abuse, the station's Honorary Medical Adviser, Dr Head, was taken afloat.

Calouste Gulbenkian was launched at 8.23 p.m. in a strong south-west gale force nine and heavy breaking seas with poor visibility. The lifeboat was to rendezvous with the container ship seven miles south-east of Hastings. During the passage heavy seas were continually breaking over the lifeboat. Almost an hour after launching, radio contact was made with *Bell Rover* and her lights were spotted.

On approaching the ship, the sick man was seen already on the pilot ladder, facing outboard, held at the shoulders by two men leaning over the bulwarks. The

Calouste Gulbenkian on the promenade at Llandudno while on relief in August 1989. (Nicholas Leach)

wind had increased and waves were reaching 30ft in height. Coxswain/Mechanic Joe Martin took the lifeboat straight in to the ship, approaching the ladder with the lifeboat's port bow. The ship appeared to have stopped in the water and was rolling heavily.

With the lifeboat's port bow pinned against the ship's starboard side, Second Coxswain Douglas White, Dr Head and another crew member waited for the ship to roll so they could grab the sick man into the forward well. As the two vessels rolled, the man was taken on board despite the movement of the vessels. Once on board, Coxswain/Mechanic Martin reversed the lifeboat away from the ship. However, as the lifeboat came astern *Bell Rover* rolled heavily onto her, damaging her port side fittings, but she got away safely.

A course was then set for Hastings pier, and the sick man was taken aft to the shelter of the cockpit. By the time the lifeboat was beached and hauled clear, the crew were soaked to the skin due to the constant seas taken aboard which flooded the cockpit. Once ashore, the sick man and doctor were taken to a waiting ambulance.

For this rescue, the Bronze medal was awarded to Coxswain/Mechanic Martin and a Letter of Appreciation, signed by the RNLI's Director, was sent to Dr Head. Medal service certificates were presented to the rest of the crew.

Disposal

On 22 May 1991, after an inspection, *Calouste Gulbenkian* was found to be uneconomical to repair, so she was withdrawn from service, declared non-operational from 30 November 1991 and placed on the sale list. In November 1991 she was sold out of service and placed on display outside a local museum at Milford Haven Docks, Pembrokeshire, where she has been ever since.

Robert and Dorothy Hardcastle

Official Number	966
Operational Number	37-04
Year built	1962
Builder	Grove & Guttridge, Cowes
Yard No.	G&G 595
Cost	£33,000
Donor	Legacy of the late Mr Hugh Robert Hardcastle, of Boston Spa, Yorkshire.
Named	6 July 1963 at Boulmer by the Duchess of Northumberland.

Stations
Boulmer	Oct. 1962 – Mar. 1968	30/11
Filey	May 1968 – June 1991	180/22

Movements
1.1.1961 – 6.10.1962	Groves & Guttridge, Cowes (uc)
6.10.1962 – 9.10.1962	Passage to Boulmer
9.10.1962 – 31.3.1968	Boulmer (sl, withdrawn 31.3.1968 and station closed)
31.3.1968 – 18.5.1968	Harrisons Bt Yd, Amble (refit)
18.5.1968 – 24.7.1982	Filey (sl)
24.7.1982 – 18.3.1983	Harrisons Bt Yd, Amble (S, RE: twin 43hp Perkins PM4 diesels; rlvd by ON.984)
18.3.1983 – 19.3.1983	Passage to Filey

Recovery of *Robert and Dorothy Hardcastle* on the beach at Filey. Filey Brigg can be seen in the background. (From an old postcard supplied by Mark Roberts)

19.3.1983 – 5.12.1986	Filey (sl)
5.12.1986 – 3.9.1987	Robson's Bt Yd South Shields (S, rlvd by ON.1022)
3.9.1987 – 4.9.1987	Passage to Filey
4.9.1987 – 26.1.1991	Filey (sl)
26.1.1991 – 20.4.1991	Leggett's Bt Yd, Grimsby (S, rlvd by ON.977)
20.4.1991 – 7.6.1991	Filey (sl)
7.6.1991 – 8.6.1991	Passage to Amble
8.6.1991 – 25.11.1991	Marshall Branson Ltd, Amble (ER)
25.11.1991 – 25.11.1991	Passage to RNLI Depot, Poole
25.11.1991 – 13.6.1992	RNLI Depot, Poole (ER)
13.6.1992 – 15.4.1993	RNLI Depot, Poole (std)

Notable Rescues

In the early hours of 18 August 1978, *Robert and Dorothy Hardcastle* was launched to assist four persons who were cut off by the tide at the foot of 400ft-high cliffs at Bempton, near Filey. Helped by the inshore lifeboat, the lifeboatmen searched the area until the four stranded youths were spotted. By the light of parachute flares and the lifeboat's searchlight, the ILB crew reached the youths and took them on board. The two lifeboats, with the rescued persons on board, then returned to Filey. A Letter of Appreciation signed by Chief of Operations was sent to Coxswain Thomas Jenkinson and the rest of the crew.

Another notable service performed by *Robert and Dorothy Hardcastle* while at Filey took place on 20 December 1983 when she was launched to the motor vessel *Rito* in a SE near-gale and rough sea with a heavy swell. The crew of *Rito* were preparing to abandon ship, but the lifeboat made seven approaches, hampered by heavy seas, and managed to take off the first survivor. The second was taken off after two further approaches, and the third survivor after another five approaches. After another two further approaches to the vessel, the captain was eventually taken off. For this rescue the Thanks on Vellum was accorded to Coxswain Frank Jenkinson and Vellum service certificates were presented to the rest of the crew.

Robert and Dorothy Hardcastle, with superstructure painted grey, moored at Filey. (Graham Taylor)

Launch of *Robert and Dorothy Hardcastle* across the beach at Filey, in the latter years of her service, using the Talus MB-H tractor. (David Phillipson)

Disposal

Robert and Dorothy Hardcastle was sold out of service on 15 April 1993 for £1,000 to Nuclear Electric plc to be used for display purposes. She was based at the Hartlepool Information Centre, Tees Road, Hartlepool, and kept at Hartlepool Docks. She has subsequently been taken round the north of England on a low loader, being displayed at public events as a fund-raising exhibit.

The Will and Fanny Kirby

Official Number	972
Operational Number	37–05
Year built	1963
Builder	William Osborne, Littlehampton
Yard No.	WO 972
Cost	£33,000
Donor	The Mr and Mrs W.L. Kirby Benevolent Fund.
Named	21 September 1963 at Seaham Harbour by the Marchioness of Londonderry.

Stations

Seaham Harbour	Sept. 1963 – Feb. 1979	45/66
Relief	Feb. 1979 – Dec. 1982	11/8
Flamborough	Jan. 1983 – Aug. 1993	142/43

The Will and Fanny Kirby entering Bridlington harbour in April 1981, on passage to Littlehampton.
(Paul Arro)

Movements

1.9.1963 – 24.2.1979	Seaham Harbour (sl)
7.1965	Royal Agricultural Show, Stoneleigh, and Leamington Spa (dis)
24.2.1979 – 26.2.1979	Passage to Staniland's Bt Yd, Thorne (via Hartlepool, Bridlington, Hull)
2.1979 – 6.1979	Staniland's Bt Yd, Thorne
6.1979 – 20.7.1979	Dickie's Bt Yd, Bangor (S, prior to entering Relief Fleet)
20.7.1979 – 1.12.1979	Hoylake (rlvd ON.1000, 4/3)
1.12.1979 – 20.7.1980	Kirkcudbright (rlvd ON.981, 2/0)
20.7.1980 – 3.8.1980	Passage to North Sunderland (via Caledonian Canal and East Coast)
3.8.1980 – 15.11.1980	North Sunderland (rlvd ON.991: 2/0)
15.11.1980 – 15.4.1981	Redcar (rlvd ON.975: 3/5)
15.4.1981 – 20.4.1981	Passage to Littlehampton (via Bridlington)
20.4.1981 – 4.7.1982	William Osborne, Littlehampton (RE: twin 43hp Perkins PM4 diesels; hull modified for launching at Flamborough; keel depth and bilge keels increased by 3in; quick release hook fitted to the stem to assist with launching by tractor and haul-off, the only Oakley to have such a fitting)
4.7.1982 – 8.7.1982	Passage to Thorne
8.7.1982 – 16.12.1982	Staniland's Bt Yd, Thorne (std)
16.12.1982 – 19.12.1982	Passage to Blyth

19.12.1982 – 3.1.1983	Blyth (std in btho until alterations to Flamborough boathouse completed)
3.1.1983 – 5.1.1983	Flamborough (T, to assess suitability at Flamborough)
5.1.1983 – 14.7.1986	Flamborough (sl)
14.7.1986 – 30.5.1987	Leggett's Bt Yd, Grimsby (S, HR with three layers of diagonally laid planking, the only Oakley to be so modified; no relief at Flamborough as ON.1022 relief at Bridlington was considered adequate cover)
30.5.1987 – 26.3.1990	Flamborough (sl)
26.3.1990 – 6.4.1990	Flamborough (S at station)
6.4.1990 – 13.3.1991	Flamborough (sl)
13.3.1991 – 23.5.1991	Leggett's Bt Yd, Grimsby (S, without relief at Flamborough)
23.5.1991 – 25.5.1991	Passage to Flamborough
25.5.1991 – 16.8.1993	Flamborough (sl)
16.8.1993 – 16.8.1993	Passage to Grimsby
16.8.1993 – 8.6.1995	Grimsby Marina (std)

Notable Rescues

The Will and Fanny Kirby was the last lifeboat at Seaham Harbour, and while there she performed a medal-winning rescue. On 11 November 1973, a number of anglers had been cut off on the drum head at the end of the north pier of the harbour, and were in danger of being swept into the sea by the heavy seas which were continually sweeping the North Pier.

The lifeboat was launched at 4.55 p.m. under the command of Coxswain Arthur Farrington with a crew of only four due to the urgency of the situation. A very heavy run of sea inside the outer harbour was sweeping round the pier head, resulting in a confused sea with a 5ft rise and fall alongside the pier. Despite frequently being thrown clear by the surge of the confused sea and swell, with skilful seamanship and boat-handling, Coxswain Farrington succeeded in taking the lifeboat alongside.

In groups of two and three, the anglers were instructed to jump on board the lifeboat. Seas continued to sweep the pier head as this operation took place, and at one point a particularly heavy wave crashed right over the pier and on to the lifeboat. The force of water, magnified as the lifeboat was rising on a swell, completely engulfed the boat and the spray canopy over the cockpit gave way, crashing down onto the coxswain at the wheel. Despite striking his head on the engine canopy, he continued at the wheel until all eighteen anglers were saved.

At 5.30 p.m. the lifeboat landed the survivors at North Dock. Because of the adverse slipway conditions, the lifeboat was taken to Sunderland for a safe berth until the weather moderated. Coxswain Farrington had his head injury attended to in Sunderland, requiring six stitches, and he had also broken his wrist. For this rescue, the Bronze medal was awarded to Coxswain Farrington; Medal service certificates were presented to Mechanic Malcolm Maconochie and crew members Ronald Leng and Maurice Thornton.

During her spell in the Relief Fleet, *The Will and Fanny Kirby* served at several stations. While on relief duty at Hoylake in 1979, she was involved in another notable

The Will and Fanny Kirby arriving at North Landing, Flamborough in 1983. (Paul Arro)

rescue. On 20 September 1979 she was launched to go to the help of the catamaran *Truganini*, of Mostyn, anchored in shallow water on the West Hoyle Bank half a mile north of Dee Buoy, in a westerly storm gale force nine, gusting to force ten, and a very rough sea.

Launching the lifeboat in the heavy seas was extremely difficult, but once at sea she made full speed for the casualty. On reaching the scene, the casualty was found to be rolling, pitching and veering violently in the confused seas around the sandbank. The lifeboat was taken alongside and two crew members were transferred to the casualty with great difficulty. As it was too hazardous to try to take off the crew of three, *Truganini* was taken in tow. Once the towline was secured, the anchor ropes were slipped and the lifeboat pulled the casualty away from the sandbank and into the protective lee of the Point of Ayr. After a difficult tow, the casualty was secured in Mostyn harbour with all on board safe. The return journey to the station took almost two hours, in which the lifeboat covered twelve miles in very rough storm-driven seas.

For this rescue, the Bronze medal was awarded to Coxswain Thomas Henry 'Harry' Jones and the Thanks on Vellum accorded to Second Coxswain John Gordon McDermott and Crewman D.A. Dodd; Medal service certificates were presented to the remainder of the crew.

Disposal
The Will and Fanny Kirby was stored at Grimsby Marina from 16 August 1993 until 8 June 1995, when she was taken to the Chatham Historic Dockyard to become part of the National Lifeboat Collection.

Fairlight

Official Number	973
Operational Number	37-06
Year built	1963
Builder	William Osborne, Littlehampton
Yard No.	WO 973
Cost	£33,000
Donor	Legacies left by Mrs Katherine Elizabeth Wood, Cranbrook, Kent; and Mrs Florence Mary Dudman, of Fareham, Hants; also the Institution's funds.
Named	23 September 1964 by Lady Egremont, daughter of the Chairman of the RNLI Committee of Management, at Hastings.

Stations

Hastings	Aug. 1964 – May 1988	207/144
Relief	Feb. 1988 – Sept. 1989	5/0
St Ives (TSD)	Sept. 1989 – Oct. 1990	19/11
New Quay (TSD)	Jan. 1991 – Apr. 1992	3/0

The scene on the beach at Hastings during the naming ceremony of *Fairlight* in September 1964. (RNLI)

Fairlight on the launching carriage outside the lifeboat house at Hastings with the station's D class inshore lifeboat and the Fowler launching tractor. (From a postcard supplied by Mark Roberts)

Movements

29.8.1964 – 14.5.1988	Hastings (sl)
14.5.1988 – 21.6.1989	FBM Marine Ltd, Cowes (S)
21.6.1989 – 16.9.1989	Hastings (rlvd ON.1125: 5/0)
16.9.1989 – 21.9.1989	Passage to St Ives
21.9.1989 – 25.10.1990	St Ives (TSD)
25.10.1990 – 26.10.1990	Passage to Marine Port Services, Pembroke Dock (via Padstow)
26.10.1990 – 26.1.1991	Marine Port Services, Pembroke Dock (S)
26.1.1991 – 27.1.1991	Passage to New Quay (Dyfed)
27.1.1991 – 11.4.1992	New Quay (Dyfed) (TSD, replaced ON.961: 3/0)
11.4.1992 – 22.4.1992	Marine Port Services, Pembroke Dock (std)
22.4.1992 – 23.4.1992	Passage to RNLI Depot, Poole
23.4.1992 – 12.10.1994	RNLI Depot, Poole (std)

Notable Rescues

Although *Fairlight* performed many services while at Hastings, during her time on station no rescues were performed for which a medal was awarded. However, a Letter of Appreciation signed by the RNLI Deputy Director and Chief of Operations was sent to the station for two rescues performed in July 1987.

The first of these took place on 19 July after the Coastguard had informed the station's Honorary Secretary that the yacht *Octopus*, of the Netherlands, was suffering engine failure in adverse conditions off Rye Harbour. *Fairlight* was launched at 2.18 p.m. to the yacht, which had five people on board and whose skipper was exhausted. At 3.06 p.m. the lifeboat reached the casualty, which was eight miles east-north-east of the station. The Rye Harbour ILB was already on scene, and had put a lifeboat man on board the yacht to assist the skipper. The ILB transferred four people to *Fairlight*, after which the yacht was towed to Rye Harbour where, at 2.58 p.m., she was secured and the survivors were landed. *Fairlight* then returned to station and was re-housed.

The second rescue took place on 29 July. *Fairlight* was launched at 7.18 a.m. to the yacht *Marna Jane*, six miles south-east of Hastings, which had engine failure and a jammed mainsail. The lifeboat reached the casualty at 8.16 a.m., and the ILB took the two crew off who were exhausted and in need of medical attention. *Fairlight* towed the yacht to Rye Harbour, and anchored her off Rye to await the tide. The ILB remained with the casualty until there was sufficient water to tow her into the harbour. At 9.40 a.m. the lifeboat returned to her station and was re-housed.

Disposal

Fairlight was sold on 12 October 1994 to Marine Salvage, Norwich, to where she was transported on 20 October 1994. She was subsequently moved to Blakeney, Norfolk, from where she was operated as a fishing boat. She retained her original name, *Fairlight*, while her engine canopy was painted grey. In August 1998, she was at Wells-next-the-Sea participating in a rally of ex-lifeboats, at which time her engine canopy was white, but she remains largely unaltered.

Returning from exercise in January 1990, *Fairlight* in the harbour at St Ives during her brief spell in Cornwall. (Tony Smith)

Jane Hay

Official Number	974
Operational Number	37–07
Year built	1963
Builder	William Osborne, Littlehampton
Yard No.	WO 974
Cost	£33,000
Donor	Legacies of Mrs Mabel Erskine, Hove, Sussex, in memory of her late husband Commander David Victor Fairfax Erskine; Mrs Anne Macdonald Smith, Dundee; and gifts from Miss Emma Smith, Dundee, and Miss Margaret Gillespie, Glasgow.
Named	17 April 1965 by Lady Morgan, niece of the late Jane Hay, at St Abbs.

Stations

St Abbs	Nov. 1964 – July 1974	20/8
Reserve	July 1974 – May 1980	30/12
Newcastle (Down)	May 1980 – Aug. 1992	70/13

Jane Hay on trials just after being completed by William Osborne's boatyard. (RNLI)

Movements

11.1964 – 12.7.1974	St Abbs (sl)
12.7.1974 – 22.9.1974	William Osborne, Littlehampton (S)
22.9.1974 – 2.1.1975	Hastings (rlvd ON.973: 7/8)
2.1.1975 – 2.7.1976	St Ives (rlvd ON.992: 13/2)
2.7.1976 – 14.12.1976	Ilfracombe (rlvd ON.986: 1/0)
15.12.1976 – 5.3.1977	Falmouth Bt Co., Falmouth (S)
5.3.1977 – 12.3.1977	Passage to Bridlington
12.3.1977 – 28.11.1977	Bridlington (rlvd ON.980: 7/2)
28.11.1977 – 29.11.1977	Passage overland to Birkenhead
29.11.1977 – 30.11.1977	Ocean Fleet's Bt Yd, Birkenhead
30.11.1977 – 1.12.1977	Passage to Donaghadee
1.12.1977 – 12.12.1977	Donaghadee (T at Newcastle and Clogher Head)
12.12.1977 – 31.12.1977	Holyhead Bt Yd (std)
31.12.1977 – 30.6.1978	Kilmore Quay (rlvd ON.997: 1/0)
1.7.1978 – 23.9.1978	Holyhead Bt Yd (S)
23.9.1978 – 25.2.1979	Port Erin (rlvd ON.998: 0/0)
26.2.1979 – 24.6.1979	New Quay (rlvd ON.996: 0/0)
24.6.1979-26.7.1979	Holyhead Bt Yd (S)
26.7.1979 – 30.7.1979	Passage to Bangor, Northern Ireland
30.7.1979 – 7.5.1980	Bangor Sh Yd, Northern Ireland (S)
7.5.1980 – 11.5.1980	Passage to Newcastle (Down)
11.5.1980 – 28.7.1985	Newcastle (Down) (sl)
28.7.1985 – 6.3.1986	Bangor Sh Yd, Northern Ireland (S)
6.3.1986 – 1.8.1988	Newcastle (Down) (sl)
1.8.1988 – 2.8.1988	Passage to Holyhead
2.8.1988 – 13.5.1989	Holyhead Bt Yd, Anglesey; Crescent Marine, Otterham Quay (S)
13.5.1989 – 16.5.1989	Passage to Newcastle (Down) (via Holyhead to Fleetwood 13.5.89; Fleetwood to Ramsey 14.5.89; Ramsey to Douglas 15.5.89; Douglas to Newcastle 16.5.89)
16.5.1989 – 4.8.1992	Newcastle (Down) (sl)
4.8.1992 – 5.8.1992	Passage to Arklow
5.8.1992	Tyrrells Bt Yd, Arklow (R, std)

Notable Rescues

During 1974, while *Jane Hay* was on relief duty at Hastings, two services were undertaken for which medals were awarded to the lifeboatmen involved. The first took place on 27 September 1974, when the lifeboat went to a fishing boat in distress 2½ miles south-west of Rye Harbour. A south-westerly gale, force nine, was gusting to storm force ten at times, with 15ft breaking seas on the beach.

Jane Hay was launched at 8.36 a.m. in the worst conditions in which a carriage launch has ever been attempted at the station. She headed towards the area where the casualty had been seen and began searching. A long search followed until, at 11.50 a.m., an RAF helicopter homed the lifeboat towards the casualty and at 12.42 p.m. the

Jane Hay in the harbour at Newcastle approaching the lifeboat house to be recovered. (Colin Watson)

lifeboat arrived on the scene. The helicopter returned to station as the cloud base was very low and conditions for operating were bad. By now the wind was storm force eleven, with 40ft seas breaking over the casualty, the motor fishing vessel *Simon Peter*, of Rye.

The lifeboat approached the fishing vessel but the three crew on board were too exhausted to move. A second approach was made during which the lifeboat was placed alongside the anchored *Simon Peter*. Second Coxswain George Douglas leant across both boats to make the headrope fast. Two of the fishing vessel's exhausted crew were then dragged bodily into the lifeboat. The skipper followed, and as soon as he was aboard the headrope was cut away and the lifeboat's engines put full astern.

The lifeboat returned to her station and was recovered quickly and efficiently, despite the breaking seas. For this rescue, the Silver medal was awarded to Coxswain/Mechanic John Martin, and the Bronze medal to Second Coxswain George White. The Thanks on Vellum was accorded to Assistant Mechanic Harry Benton, Second Assistant Mechanic Robert Shoesmith and crew members Richard Adams, Michael Barrow, Albert White and Richard Read. A framed letter of thanks was sent to Head Launcher Ronald White.

The second service took place less than three months later. On 23 December 1974 *Jane Hay* was launched to the Argentinian warship *Candido de Lasala*, on board which had been an explosion and medical help was needed. The wind was south–easterly force five, with a moderate sea. The lifeboat took out Dr Peter Davy (honorary medical advisor).

After reaching the warship, *Jane Hay* was joined by Rescue Helicopter 41 and Dr Davy was asked to transfer to the helicopter for a quicker transit to the ship. The lifeboat steered at full speed into the wind, and the helicopter crewman was lowered on board, landing safely after several attempts. While he was putting Dr Davy into the other strop, the helicopter lost contact with the lifeboat. Both men were dragged off the deck with a pendulum motion, smashing back into the lifeboat stern before being separated in the water.

While the helicopter was repositioned, Dr Davy drifted away but was then recovered and taken onto *Candido de Lasala*. The injured men were tended and one was transferred by helicopter to hospital with the doctor in company. On arrival, and only after ensuring that the injured man was being cared for, Dr Davy allowed himself to be examined by another doctor. He was found to have seven broken ribs and must have been in great pain throughout the service. For his efforts, Dr Davy was awarded the Silver medal.

Disposal

Jane Hay was stored at Arklow Marine & Leisure Ltd, Arklow, from 5 December 1992 until being dismantled and broken up in Summer 1995.

Sir James Knott

Official Number	975
Operational Number	37–08
Year built	1963
Builder	Grove & Guttridge, Cowes
Yard No.	G&G 604
Cost	£33,000
Donor	Sir James Knott Trust, and RNLI General Funds.
Named	6 June 1964 at Cullercoats by Her Grace the Duchess of Northumberland.

Sir James Knott on trials after being built, ready to go to Cullercoats. (From a postcard supplied by Mark Roberts)

Sir James Knott arriving at Redcar for the first time, on 28 November 1972, where she served until the mid-1980s. (David Phillipson)

Stations

Cullercoats	Nov. 1963 – May 1969	16/14
Relief	May 1969 – Nov. 1972	5/4
Redcar	Nov. 1972 – Mar. 1986	78/63
Relief	Mar. 1986 – May 1989	28/0

Movements

15.6.1962 – 16.11.1963	Groves & Guttridge, Cowes (uc; 100th lifeboat built at this yard)
21.11.1963 – 4.5.1969	Cullercoats (sl)
4.5.1969 – 10.5.1969	Passage to Anstruther
10.5.1969 – 1.10.1971	Anstruther (rlvd ON.983: 5/4)
1.10.1971 – 1.11.1972	No record
28.11.1972 – 12.4.1978	Redcar (sl; rededicated 28.5.1973, service performed by Lord Bishop of Whitby and Right Reverend J. Yates)
12.4.1978 – 15.6.1978	Harrison Bt Yd, Amble (S and radar installed funded by a local appeal in Redcar, rlvd by ON.979 at Redcar)
15.6.1978 – 20.5.1979	Redcar (sl)
20.5.1979 – 22.7.1979	Harrison Bt Yd, Amble (rlvd by ON.942)
22.7.1979 – 16.11.1980	Redcar (sl)
16.11.1980 – 5.6.1981	Harrison Bt Yd, Amble (S, R, rlvd by ON.972)
5.6.1981 – 14.7.1985	Redcar (sl)
14.7.1985 – 21.3.1986	Harrison Bt Yd, Amble (S, fitted with folding wh, part of hull replanked)

21.3.1986 – 23.3.1986	Passage to Scarborough (via Hartlepool)
23.3.1986 – 25.4.1987	Scarborough (rlvd ON.979: 12/0)
25.4.1987 – 26.4.1987	Passage to Amble (via Hartlepool)
26.4.1987 – 26.4.1987	Harrison Bt Yd, Amble (I)
26 4.1987 – 4.5.1987	Eyemouth Bt Co., Eyemouth (Alts)
4.5.1987 – 30.7.1988	Anstruther (rlvd ON.983: 12/0)
30.7.1988 – 31.7.1988	Passage to Newcastle (via Port St Mary)
31.7.1988 – 6.3.1989	Newcastle (rlvd ON.974)
6.3.1989 – 6.5.1989	Harrison Bt Yd, Amble
6.5.1989 – 17.5.1989	Newcastle (rlvd ON.974: 4/0)
17.5.1989 – 18.5.1989	Passage to Bangor (via Port St Mary)
18.5.1989 – 1.4.1990	Dickie's Bt Yd, Bangor (I, Std)

Notable Rescues

The first service undertaken by *Sir James Knott* took place on 17 November 1963, while on her delivery passage from Cowes to Cullercoats. She was called to help a motor cruiser one mile north of Gorleston, from which she saved two people and towed the cruiser safely into Gorleston.

Many of her rescues at Redcar were of a routine nature. She often helped fishing cobles that got into difficulty when operating out of Redcar and Middlesbrough. However, on 12 November 1982, she performed a particularly fine service to the fishing boat *Lady Theresa*, of Middlesbrough.

Sir James Knott arriving at Scarborough for relief duties on 23 March 1986, having just been replaced at Redcar. (David Phillipson)

Sir James Knott at Amble Boatyard in August 1995 after disposal by the RNLI. (Nicholas Leach)

The boat was in a rough sea about one mile north-east of the lifeboat station and a gale to strong gale, force eight to nine, was blowing from the south-west when, just after midday, she fired signals of distress. *Sir James Knott* was soon launched under the command of Coxswain David Buckworth. Just over ten minutes later, Coxswain Buckworth brought the lifeboat alongside the fishing boat and was able to safely take the four occupants on board. A tow was then rigged and the casualty was beached at Redcar at 12.50 p.m.

For this service a Letter of Appreciation signed by the RNLI Director, Rear Admiral W.J. Graham, was sent to Coxswain Buckworth and the crew. In the letter, the Director commended all of the lifeboatmen on their vigilance, speed and efficiency on this occasion.

Disposal

Sir James Knott was stored at Dickie's Boat Yard, Bangor, from 18 May 1989, and on 1 November 1989 was placed on the RNLI sale list. Since 1 April 1990 she has been permanently loaned to the Langburgh-on-Tees Museum Service for display at Kirkleatham Old Hall Museum, Redcar. During the summer of 1995 she was repainted at Amble Bt Yd, Amble, for display. On 26 June 1999 she went on display for the third season at the museum, and remains at the Museum as an interesting exhibit with local interest.

Lilly Wainwright

Official Number	976
Operational Number	37–09
Year built	1964
Builder	Groves & Guttridge, Cowes
Yard No.	G&G 605
Cost	£33,000
Donor	Legacy of Mr J.H. Wainwright, gift from the Arthur Jowett Fund plus RNLI General Funds.
Named	15 May 1964 by HRH Princess Marina, Duchess of Kent, at Llandudno.

Stations

Llandudno	30 Jan. 1964 – 23 Nov. 1990	124/58
Kilmore Quay	25 Jan. 1991 – 2 Dec. 1992	11/2

Movements

15.6.1962 – 25.1.1964	Groves & Guttridge, Cowes (uc)
2.2.1964 – 7.7.1978	Llandudno (sl)
7.7.1978 – 2.3.1979	Dickie's Bt Yd, Bangor (rlvd by ON.994)
2.3.1979 – 4.3.1979	Passage to Llandudno
4.3.1979 – 20.11.1984	Llandudno (sl)
27.11.1984 – 23.7.1985	Dickie's Bt Yd, Bangor (S, rlvd by ON.994)
23.7.1985 – 18.10.1985	Llandudno (sl)
8.10.1985 – 26.10.1985	Dickie's Bt Yd, Bangor (R, rlvd by ON.942)
26.10.1985 – 23.5.1988	Llandudno (sl)
23.5.1988 – 26.5.1988	Passage overland to Cowes
26.5.1988 – 30.11.1989	FBM Marine, Cowes (S, hull rebuilt, rlvd by ON.961)

Lilly Wainwright being taken through the streets in Llandudno from the lifeboat house to the promenade. (Jeff Morris)

30.11.1989 – 8.12.1989	RNLI Depot, Poole (at Salterns Marina, vibration on main engines; due to be transported overland to Holyhead Bt Yd for lifting in and sailing to Llandudno)
8.12.1989 – 11.12.1989	Passage overland to Bangor
11.12.1989 – 18.12.1989	Dickie's Bt Yd, Bangor
18.12.1989 – 24.11.1990	Llandudno (sl)
24.11.1990 – 26.11.1990	Llandudno (ER, new lifeboat ON.1164 at Llandudno)
26.11.1990 – 25.1.1991	Tyrell's Bt Yd, Arklow (S)
25.1.1991 – 1.2.1993	Kilmore Quay (TSD)
1.2.1993 – 30.9.1993	Crosshaven Bt Yd, Cork (ER, std)

Notable Rescues

On 4 August 1977, *Lilly Wainwright* was launched to go to the assistance of the yacht *Dyllys*, which was in difficulties twelve miles north of Llandudno. The lifeboat was driven through extremely rough seas in a force eight south-westerly gale, accompanied by torrential rain which reduced visibility. Almost four hours after launching, the lifeboat reached the casualty.

Already on the scene was the Royal Fleet Auxiliary vessel *White Rover*, which was standing by and provided a lee for the lifeboat to manoeuvre towards the yacht. When close enough, the lifeboatmen threw across a line which was secured by the yacht's crew. Slowly, the tow began while *White Rover* continued on her way.

At 11.10 p.m. the lifeboat and yacht arrived in Llandudno Bay, but as no suitable mooring was available and weather forecasts indicated the gale force winds would veer to the north-west, it was decided to tow the yacht round the Great Orme to Deganwy. Here, the yacht was safely moored in the early hours of 5 August, after

Lilly Wainwright on the promenade at Llandudno, a common sight during the summer. (From a postcard supplied by David Gooch)

Lilly Wainwright on the beach at Clogher Head.

which the lifeboat returned to her station. Lilly Wainwright was beached just after 3.00 a.m. having been on service for almost twelve hours.

For this rescue, in which the yacht and its two occupants had been saved, a Letter of Appreciation signed by the RNLI's Director was sent to Coxswain Meurig Davies and the crew of the lifeboat.

Disposal

Lilly Wainwright was sold out of service on 30 September 1993 for £1,000 to the Cobh Heritage Trust Ltd, Ireland, minus her engines. She was subsequently sold into private hands and transferred to Verolme Shipyard, Cork, where she remained out of the water for a number of years. In 2001, she was surveyed for possible use on the Irish inland waterway system.

Charles Fred Grantham

Official Number	977
Operational Number	37-10
Year built	1964
Builder	Groves & Guttridge, Cowes
Yard No.	G&G 606
Cost	£33,000
Donor	Legacies of Mrs Elizabeth Wright Montford, Market Drayton and Miss Edith Mary Dearden, Hyde, Cheshire.
Named	Named after former Honorary Secretary, Charles Fred Grantham, on 9 July 1964 by his son, Admiral Sir Guy Grantham GCB, CBE, DSO, former Governor and Commander-in-Chief of Malta, at Skegness.

Stations

Skegness	Apr. 1964 – Aug. 1990	148/96
Scarborough	Oct. 1990 – Jan. 1991	5/4
Relief	Jan. 1991 – July 1992	1/0

Movements

15.6.1962 – 17.4.1964	Groves & Guttridge, Cowes (uc)
17.4.1964 – 20.4.1964	Passage to Skegness
20.4.1964 – 29.9.1977	Skegness (sl)
29.9.1977 – 2.10.1977	Passage to Oulton Broad
2.10.1977 – 16.4.1978	Fletchers Bt Yd, Lowestoft (S, rlvd by ON.961)
16.4.1978 – 18.4.1978	Passage to Skegness
18.4.1978 – 16.9.1979	Skegness (sl)
16.9.1979 – 14.10.1979	Fletchers Bt Yd, Lowestoft (S, rlvd by ON.961)
14.10.1979 – 25.7.1983	Skegness (sl)
25.7.1983 – 21.7.1984	Fletchers Bt Yd, Lowestoft (S, rlvd by ON.961)
21.7.1984 – 28.9.1986	Skegness (sl)
28.9.1986 – 26.3.1988	Whisstocks Bt Yd, Woodbridge (S and hull replanked, rlvd by ON.984)
26.3.1988 – 27.3.1988	Passage to Skegness
27.3.1988 – 9.8.1990	Skegness (sl)
9.8.1990 – 9.10.1990	Leggett's Bt Yd, Grimsby (withdrawn from station)
9.10.1990 – 26.1.1991	Scarborough (TSD: 5/4)
26.1.1991 – 20.4.1991	Filey (relieving ON.966: 1/0)
20.4.1991 – 21.4.1991	Bridlington (std overnight)
21.4.1991 – 25.4.1991	Leggett's Bt Yd, Grimsby (ER)
25.4.1991 – 25.4.1991	Passage overland to Salterns Marina
26.4.1991 – 26.4.1991	Passage to Branksea Marine, Wareham
26.4.1991 – 20.8.1993	Branksea Marine, Ridge, Wareham (std, then broken up)

Seen in her early years, *Charles Fred Grantham* with a grey engine casing, open aft cockpit and no radar. (From a postcard in the author's collection)

Charles Fred Grantham at Gorleston while on passage in 1970. (John Markham)

Launch of *Charles Fred Grantham* across the beach at Skegness watched by a large crowd, possibly during the station's annual Lifeboat Day. (From a postcard in the author's collection)

Notable Rescue

On 2 December 1972, *Charles Fred Grantham* was launched from Skegness in driving rain, heavy seas and high winds to search for the fishing vessel *Silver Surf*, of Fosdyke, which had been reported overdue. Under the command of Coxswain Ken Holland, the lifeboat was taken through the Wainfleet Swatchway to the Boston deeps, where it was thought the *Silver Surf* might be found.

Once on the scene, the lifeboatmen began searching, a task made difficult because of the driving spray thrown by the heavy seas. The fishing vessel's mast was soon spotted on the opposite side of the Long Sand, approximately five miles south-west of the Lynn Well lightship. The lifeboat was taken through the Parlour Channel to reach her and, with an RAF helicopter also in attendance, went alongside. The fishing vessel was rolling heavily in the rough seas and had her propellers fouled by the boat's own fishing nets.

Once alongside, a towline was passed and the *Silver Surf*, on which was a crew of two, was towed up the River Welland to the landing stage at Fosdyke. Not only had the nets fouled the propeller, but the anchor would not hold and both anchors had been lost before the lifeboat had arrived on the scene.

Had the lifeboat not arrived when it did, the *Silver Surf* would have been dashed to pieces on the Long Sand. It was one of the most testing services performed by *Charles Fred Grantham*, after which Coxswain Holland said: 'This launch was a severe test for the lifeboat, and she handled admirably in the hazardous conditions.'

Disposal

Charles Fred Grantham was placed on the sale list on 11 July 1992; in 1993, she was broken up at Branksea Marine.

The Royal Thames

Official Number	978
Operational Number	37-11
Year built	1964
Builder	J.S. White, Cowes
Yard No.	W 5542
Cost	£31,749
Donor	Legacy of Mr Douglas Alfred Forster, Maidstone, Kent; gifts from Mr G.J.F. Jackson, Duffield Place, Hampshire, and Miss Gladys Ellison, Eastbourne; and RNLI funds.
Named	14 July 1964 by the Honourable Mrs Valentine Wyndham-Quin.

Stations

Caister	Feb. 1964 – Oct. 1969	30/15
Runswick	Sept. 1970 – Jan. 1978	38/30
Pwllheli	May 1979 – Jan. 1991	32/7
Clogher Head	Mar. 1991 – Mar. 1993	5/0

The Royal Thames off Caister beach in August 1964. She was the last RNLI lifeboat to serve at Caister. (Jeff Morris)

The Royal Thames outside the lifeboat house at Pwllheli, her final station. (David Phillipson)

Movements

21.2.1964 – 17.10.1969	Caister (sl)
17.10.1969 – 20.9.1970	Harrison Bt Yd, Amble (S)
20.9.1970 – 30.6.1978	Runswick (sl)
30.6.1978 – 5.4.1979	Harrison Bt Yd, Amble (S, std)
5.4.1979 – 7.4.1979	Passage overland to Dickie's Bt Yd, Bangor
7.4.1979 – 16.5.1979	Dickie's Bt Yd, Bangor (S)
16.5.1979 – 18.5.1979	Passage to Pwllheli (DI aboard)
18.5.1979 – 5.5.1983	Pwllheli (sl)
5.5.1983 – 16.12.1983	Dickie's Bt Yd, Bangor (S, rlvd by ON. 942)
16.12.1983 – 1.1.1988	Pwllheli (sl)
1.1.1988 – 25.8.1988	FBM Marine Ltd, Cowes (S)
25.8.1988 – 31.8.1988	RNLI Depot, Poole (ER)
31.8.1988 – 26.1.1991	Pwllheli (sl)
26.1.1991 – 29.3.1991	Tyrells Bt Yd, Arklow (std)
29.3.1991 – 20.10.1991	Clogher Head (TSD)
20.10.1991 – 30.11.1991	Tyrells Bt Yd, Arklow (S)
30.11.1991 – 8.3.1993	Clogher Head (TSD)
8.3.1993 – 19.3.1993	Dickie's Bt Yd, Bangor
19.3.1993 – 22.3.1993	Passage overland to Poole
22.3.1993 – 12.10.1994	RNLI Depot, Poole (std, for disposal)

The Royal Thames outside the lifeboat house at Runswick. She was the last lifeboat to serve at this station, which was closed in 1978 when an Atlantic 21 was stationed at the nearby village of Staithes. (David Phillipson)

The Royal Thames at Pwllheli after being fitted with radar. (RNLI)

Notable Rescues

While she was serving at Caister, *The Royal Thames* was involved in a notable rescue while working with the neighbouring Great Yarmouth & Gorleston lifeboat. At 8.00 p.m. on 22 June 1967 it was learned that an RAF helicopter had crashed about half a mile south of the lifeboat station. *The Royal Thames* was launched at 8.05 p.m. in a moderate to fresh south-westerly breeze and a moderate sea. The coxswain at Great Yarmouth & Gorleston was informed and both the lifeboat, *Louise Stephens*, and inshore lifeboat were launched to assist.

On reaching the area where the helicopter had crashed, the crew of *The Royal Thames* were informed that a fishing boat had recovered the body of one of the three men on board the helicopter. The body was transferred to the Caister lifeboat which then continued to search for the missing men. Various items of equipment were recovered by the Caister lifeboat and Great Yarmouth & Gorleston IRB, but no trace was found of the two missing men. *The Royal Thames* returned to Caister at 9.25 p.m. and *Louise Stephens* to Gorleston at 10.15 p.m. The tractor at Caister was used on 23 June to assist with the recovery of the wreckage.

Following this service, a letter of sympathy was sent by the RNLI to RAF Coltishall and letters of thanks for the services rendered were received by the Institution from RAF Coltishall and HQ, No.18 Group RAF at Pitreavie Castle.

After service at Caister, *The Royal Thames* was transferred to Runswick where she was often called out to escort and help the local fishing cobles. When she was launched on 30 August 1975, with Coxswain Harold Armstrong in command, to two of the local cobles that were in danger off Staithes, a particularly fine service was performed.

The wind was north-easterly force four with poor visibility, but conditions off Staithes, a nearby village from which the cobles were operating, were deteriorating. On reaching the scene, *The Royal Thames* first escorted the coble *Deep Harmony* through broken water into Staithes harbour. She had twelve passengers and one crewman on board. *The Royal Thames* then returned to sea and approached the other coble, *Golden Days*, which was about 1½ miles off Port Mulgrave with eight passengers and one crewman on board.

The coble was encountering heavy seas which were causing her some difficulty as the lifeboat came alongside. The eight passengers were then taken off and Second Coxswain Nigel Hinchley was put on board the coble. As conditions had worsened even further, the coble headed for Runswick escorted by the lifeboat. Once they reached the village, the eight people were landed and the coble moored.

Disposal

During 1993, *The Royal Thames* remained in the partially dismantled old lifeboat house following her replacement at Clogher Head by a new 12m Mersey, until she was taken to Dickie's Bt Yd, Bangor, for storage. She was then stored at RNLI Depot, Poole, from 22 March 1993 to 12 October 1994, awaiting disposal, having been declared non-operational on 12 October 1994. She was sold as scrap to Marine Salvage, Norwich, and was transported to Norfolk on 20 October 1994. She was later kept out of the water at Hewitt's Bt Yd, Blakeney.

James and Catherine MacFarlane/Amelia

Official Number	979
Operational Number	37–12
Year built	1964
Builder	J.S. White, Cowes
Yard No.	W 5543
Cost	£33,000
Donor	Legacy of Mr Robert F. MacFarlane, of Messrs MacFarlane & Lang Co. Ltd.
Named	James and Catherine MacFarlane on 26 May 1964 at Cowes. In 1967, appropriated to the legacy of Mrs A. Borland, and RNLI funds, and renamed *Amelia*.

Stations

Relief★	1964 – 1978	43/12
Scarborough	Nov. 1978 – Sept. 1991	116/18

★This lifeboat was the first one to be built specifically for service in tshe Reserve (subsequently Relief) Fleet.

Movements

1.5.1964 – 24.5.1965	Passage, trials, then placed in Reserve Fleet 5.1964
24.5.1965 – 30.11.1965	Scarborough (rlvd ON.942: 3/0)
30.11.1965 – 1.7.1966	Sheringham (rlvd ON.960: 2/0)
1.7.1966 – 2.8.1968	Seaham harbour (rlvd ON.972: 1/2)
2.8.1968 – 9.6.1969	Bridlington (rlvd ON.980: 2/0)
9.6.1969 – 19.7.1969	Skegness (rlvd ON.977: 1/0)
19.7.1969 – 1.12.1970	Wells (rlvd ON.982: 1/0)
1.12.1970 – 8.4.1971	Clacton-on-Sea (rlvd ON.985, 4/0)
8.4.1971 – 15.7.1971	North Sunderland (rlvd ON.991: 1/0)
15.7.1971 – 15.11.1971	Newbiggin (rlvd ON.984: 1/0)
15.11.1971 – 2.4.1973	J.S. White, Cowes (ER, std)
2.4.1973 – 10.4.1973	Passage to Sennen Cove
10.4.1973 – 31.12.1973	Sennen Cove (rlvd ON.856 and ON.999: 5/2)
31.12.1973 – 1.8.1975	Runswick (rlvd ON.978, 4/0)
21.5.1975	Attended naming ceremony of Whitby lifeboat *The White Rose of Yorkshire*, on relief duty at Runswick
1.8.1975 – 1.8.1976	Redcar (rlvd ON.975: 4/0)
1.8.1976 – 12.3.1977	North Sunderland (rlvd ON.991: 4/5)
12.3.1977 – 15.7.1977	Filey (rlvd ON.966: 2/0)
15.7.1977 – 1.3.1978	Newbiggin (rlvd ON.984: 2/3)
10.3.1978 – 11.4.1978	Seaham (rlvd ON.972: 1/0)
11.4.1978 – 15.6.1978	Redcar (rlvd ON.975:0/0)
15.6.1978 – 8.11.1978	Seaham (rlvd ON.972)
8.11.1978 – 25.3.1980	Scarborough (sl)
25.3.1980 – 26.3.1980	Passage to Amble
26.3.1980 – 14.4.1980	Harrison Bt Yd, Amble (S, rlvd by ON.942)
14.4.1980 – 15.4.1980	Passage to Scarborough
15.4.1980 – 20.3.1983	Scarborough (sl)
20.3.1983 – 21.3.1983	Passage to Amble

Named *James and Catherine MacFarlane*, displayed at the Royal Show, Stoneleigh, on 9 July 1964. (Jeff Morris)

21.3.1983 – 16.12.1983	Harrison Bt Yd, Amble (S, rlvd by ON.984, fixed wh fitted over cockpit)
16.12.1983 – 17.12.1983	Passage to Scarborough
17.12.1983 – 23.2.1986	Scarborough (sl)
23.2.1986 – 24.2.1986	Passage to South Shields
24.2.1986 – 23.4.1987	Robson's Bt Yd South Shields (S, rlvd by ON.975)
23.4.1987 – 24.4.1987	Passage to Scarborough
24.4.1987 – 10.10.1990	Scarborough (sl)
10.10.1990 – 24.1.1991	Leggett's Bt Yd, Grimsby (S)
24.1.1991 – 1.10.1991	Scarborough (sl, withdrawn 27.9.1991, but remained at station)
1.10.1991 – 12.2.1992	Leggett's Bt Yd, Grimsby (std, ER)

Notable Rescue

On 23 January 1984, *The Will and Fanny Kirby* was launched from the North Landing at Flamborough to escort three Bridlington cobles in a near gale force seven and rough sea with heavy swell. With conditions rapidly deteriorating, it was decided to escort the cobles to Scarborough, and the lifeboat *Amelia* from Scarborough was launched to assist. As conditions made it impossible to enter Scarborough harbour safely due to the heavy surf that was running, the cobles and lifeboats made for Whitby, which was reached safely.

Once the cobles were safe, *Amelia* and *The Will and Fanny Kirby* then left Whitby and headed south. As *The Will and Fanny Kirby* could not safely get back to her station at North Landing, both boats made for Scarborough. Here, despite extremely heavy surf, *Amelia* cautiously approached and successfully entered the harbour. Using the same approach, however, *The Will and Fanny Kirby* was caught by a heavy breaking sea, estimated to be 20-25ft high, which struck the boat's starboard side knocking her by about 120 degrees over to port and the engine cut-out switches operated. The coxswain was thrown off the wheel, but he regained it as the lifeboat righted. Before the engines could be restarted, though, the boat was knocked down again and one crew member was washed overboard, but regained the boat. In all, five consecutive heavy seas knocked the lifeboat down to port before it was possible to restart the engines and enter the harbour.

Letters of Appreciation signed by the Director were sent to Coxswain James Major, the crew of the Flamborough lifeboat, and to Coxswain Ian Firman and the crew of the Scarborough lifeboat. The Flamborough coxswain and crew expressed their delight with the way that *The Will and Fanny Kirby* had taken them through. On inspection it was found that she had sustained virtually no damage, despite the heavy pounding suffered.

Disposal

Amelia was stored as an emergency relief lifeboat at Leggett's Boat Yard, Grimsby, until 12 February 1992. She was then sold for £2,000 to Charlestown Enterprises, Carlyon Bay, Cornwall. She left the RNLI Depot, Poole, on 3 March 1992 and was taken overland to Charlestown, where she was placed on permanent display outside the Shipwreck & Heritage Museum. She has been displayed there ever since.

Amelia at Scarborough in the latter days of her service career, at sea for the station's annual Lifeboat Day. (David Phillipson)

William Henry and Mary King

Official Number	980
Operational Number	37-13 (number never displayed on boat)
Year built	1964
Builder	J.S. White, Cowes
Yard No.	W 5544
Cost	£33,000
Donor	Legacy of Miss Jane Graham King, Sutton, Surrey; in memory of her father and mother, plus RNLI funds.
Named	8 July 1965 by HRH Princess Marina, Duchess of Kent, at Cromer.

Stations
Cromer No.2	Oct. 1964 – June 1967	12/1
Bridlington	Sept. 1967 – Jan. 1989	291★/83
North Sunderland	Mar. 1989 – Aug. 1990	9/0

★Including one service carried out while on passage.

Movements
24.10.1964 – 22.6.1967	Cromer No.2 (sl)
22.6.1967 – 1.9.1967	Harrison Bt Yd, Amble (S, re-allocated to Bridlington)
1.9.1967 – 2.9.1967	Passage to Bridlington

William Henry and Mary King on the beach at Cromer outside the No.2 lifeboat house. She served as the second lifeboat at Cromer until June 1967, when an inshore lifeboat was sent to the station in her place. (MPL)

2.9.1967 – 6.6.1981	Bridlington (sl)
1977	Radar installed
6.6.1981 – 7.6.1981	Passage to Amble
7.6.1981 – 22.11.1981	Harrison Bt Yd, Amble (S, rlvd by ON.984)
22.11.1981 – 17.9.1985	Bridlington (sl)
17.9.1985 – 18.9.1985	Passage to South Shields
18.9.1985 – 20.9.1985	Robson's Bt Yd, South Shields (R)
20.9.1985 – 21.9.1985	Passage to Bridlington
21.9.1985 – 21.10.1985	Bridlington (sl)
21.10.1985 – 22.10.1985	Passage to Robson's Bt Yd
22.10.1985 – 5.12.1986	Robson's Bt Yd, South Shields (HR, cost approximately £130,000; rigid wh and VHF/DF aerial fitted; rlvd by ON.867 to 19.7.86, ON.1022 from 19.7.1986; T out of Robson's Bt Yd)
5.12.1986 – 2.2.1988	Bridlington (sl)
2.2.1988 – 5.2.1988	Robson's Bt Yd, South Shields (R)
6.2.1988 – 31.1.1989	Bridlington (sl)
31.1.1989 – 1.2.1989	Whitby (rlvg ON.1131)
1.2.1989–30.3.1989	Robson's Bt Yd, South Shields (R)
30.3.1989–15.8.1990	North Sunderland (TSD)
15.8.1990–16.8.1990	North Sunderland (awaiting passage)
16.8.1990–4.10.1990	Robson's Bt Yd, South Shields (S)
4.10.1990–23.7.1991	RNLI Depot, Poole (std, for disposal)

Notable Rescues

During her service career at Bridlington, *William Henry and Mary King* was involved in several outstanding services. The first came less than a year after she was placed on station when she was involved in a service described in the official report as 'long, frustrating and hazardous'. It began at 4.34 p.m. on 4 February 1968 when she was launched under the command of Second Coxswain John Simpson to a German motor vessel in difficulties less than a mile from Bridlington harbour. With a force nine gale blowing, heavy seas continually swept over the tractor during the launch from the beach.

Once at sea, *William Henry and Mary King* made for the motor vessel *Maria F,* of Hamburg, which was dragging both anchors and had a fouled propeller. The lifeboat stood by but it was impossible to put a man aboard in the dreadful conditions. At 8.40 p.m. the lifeboat went into harbour to discuss the situation with the station's Honorary Secretary, and Coxswain John King, who had been on leave, embarked. Just after 10.00 p.m. the coaster indicated that it was disabled so the lifeboat left harbour and went out again into the heavy seas.

Coxswain King anchored the lifeboat to windward and veered down towards the casualty, but the crew refused to leave. By 12.15 a.m., the following morning, the coaster was aground and being pounded by the seas as the lifeboat continued to stand by. It was not possible to get alongside, and as the lifeboat weighed anchor the anchor cable fouled the propellers. One was cleared while at sea, an operation which involved the crew having to work under water. The other one could not be cleared, so the lifeboat was beached at 2.20 a.m. to enable it to be cleared, after which the lifeboat again launched.

Still the crew of *Maria F* refused to leave their ship but by 4.20 a.m., after the seas had gone down, the German crew were asking for help. The lifeboat managed to

William Henry and Mary King launching at Bridlington in February 1988. (Paul Russell)

William Henry and Mary King on the beach at Bridlington in 1988. (Paul Arro)

manoeuvre close in and remain alongside long enough for one member of the coaster's crew to jump. However, she fractured her arm upon landing on the lifeboat's deck, and the rest of the crew, seeing this, decided to stay on board as the ship was now afloat.

The lifeboat landed the injured woman at the harbour at 4.55 a.m., and the crew took the opportunity to have some food and a change of clothing. At 8.30 a.m. she went out to *Maria F* and brought the master ashore to contact the owner and arrange for tugs to be sent. He was returned to his vessel at 11.25 a.m., and the lifeboat stood by until the tug *Lady Alma* took over. For this rescue the Bronze medal was awarded to Coxswain John King and the Thanks on Vellum was accorded to the crew: Second Coxswain John Simpson, Bowman Denis Atkins, Mechanic Roderick Stott, Assistant Mechanic Richard Cranswick and crew members George Traves, Fred Walkington, Brian Bevan, Brian Fenton and Harry Woods.

Almost exactly four years later, *William Henry and Mary King* was involved in another medal-winning service. At 4.30 a.m. on 24 January 1972 she was launched in a force eight gale, with rough seas, to the motor fishing vessel *My Susanne*, of Bridlington. The vessel's engines had failed and she was drifting ashore under Sewerby cliffs, near Flamborough.

Once the lifeboat was on the scene, she veered towards the casualty despite being in danger of broaching. However, the lifeboat crew successfully fired a rocket over the casualty, and passed a line followed by a cable. A tow was rigged and, as the lifeboat began to pull her away, the casualty's engines were started. Although the towing cable fouled the lifeboat's port propeller, the lifeboat continued on her starboard engine. The casualty, with a crew of four, was brought into harbour. For this rescue, the Bronze medal was awarded to Coxswain John King. The remainder of the crew received medal service certificates.

Just over a year later, *William Henry and Mary King* was involved in the most notable service of her career. On the morning of 2 April 1973 she was launched to go to the aid of the coble *Calaharis* in a gale gusting to hurricane force, and a very rough sea. Once at sea, Coxswain John King learned that another fishing coble, *Mary Rose*, was also making heavy weather, so she was escorted to harbour. Then Coxswain King began the search for *Calaharis* only to be told that a motor fishing vessel, *White Knight* of Grimsby, had also broken down. The Coastguard instructed that the lifeboat go to her assistance and so the Flamborough lifeboat assisted *Calaharis*.

As she progressed towards *White Knight*, the lifeboat was swept by very heavy seas with spray reducing visibility. The search was carried out in winds up to force thirteen and visibility was so poor that the lifeboat crew could not see the flares fired from the casualty. At 12.50 p.m. *White Knight* was spotted and the lifeboat approached but it was too dangerous to lie alongside the casualty, so instead three short passes were made in extremely hazardous conditions. Two people were taken off at the first attempt, two on the second and the skipper on the third. For this rescue, the Silver medal was awarded to Coxswain King and the Thanks on Vellum was accorded to Second Coxswain George Traves, Bowman Denis Atkins, Mechanic Roderick Stott, Assistant Mechanic Anthony Ayre, Fred Walkington and Ken Bentley.

On 15 February 1979 *William Henry and Mary King* was involved in yet another medal-winning service. She launched to the cargo vessel *Sunnanhav*, of West Germany, which had broken down in a force ten to eleven storm, with driving snow and very heavy seas. In blizzard conditions the ice was re-forming on the lifeboat as quickly as it was cleared. The temperature was minus four degrees centigrade.

Shortly after leaving the shelter of Bridlington Bay, the lifeboat was informed that *Sunnanhav* had regained limited power. A mile or so further on, the lifeboat was lifted by a big sea which filled the cockpit with water and the radar went dead. A few minutes later the Coastguard informed the lifeboat that *Sunnanhav* had regained full power and was making for Humber for shelter from the still worsening seas.

During the return passage, the lifeboat was struck by a huge wave off Filey Brig and knocked down to starboard, causing the engine cut-out system to operate. The 'capsize switches' were made and the engines re-started first time. The crew, who had all been attached by lifelines, confirmed they were well and course was set for Flamborough Head. The lifeboat then proceeded to her station, where she arrived having been at sea for almost ten hours. She was re-housed with difficulty, as there were problems negotiating the carriage up the slip from the beach due to the icy conditions.

For this rescue, performed in the most difficult conditions, the Bronze medal was awarded to Coxswain Fred Walkington and Medal Service Certificates were presented to the remainder of the crew: Second Coxswain Denis Atkins, Mechanic Roderick Stott, Assistant Mechanic John Sharp, and crew members Anthony Ayre, R.W. Stork and Paul Stavely.

Disposal

Following her last inspection on 4 October 1990, *William Henry and Mary King* was stored at the RNLI Depot, Poole. She was declared non-operational on 23 July 1991, scrapped and deleted from the Register of British Ships. She was taken overland from RNLI Depot to a playground at Drayton Park Primary School, Islington, London, for use in a children's play area as part of a culture centre.

Mary Pullman

Official Number	981
Operational Number	37-14
Year built	1964
Builder	William Osborne, Littlehampton
Yard No.	WO 981
Cost	£33,000
Donor	Gift from the late Sir Derek Wheeler, Bt, in memory of his mother, whose maiden name was Mary Pullman.
Named	5 June 1965 by the Countess of Galloway, at Kirkcudbright.

Stations

Kirkcudbright	May 1965 – Apr 1989	89/34

Movements

1.1965	Earls Court Boat Show, London (dis)
2.1965	William Osborne, Littlehampton (T)
3.1965	Ayr Show (dis)
4.1965	Bull Ring, Birmingham (dis)
2.5.1965 – 3.12.1979	Kirkcudbright (sl)
3.12.1979 – 18.7.1980	Robertson's Bt Yd, Sandbank (S)
18.7.1980 – 19.7.1980	Passage to Kirkcudbright (overnight)
19.7.1980 – 7.8.1985	Kirkcudbright (sl)
7.8.1985 – 7.9.1985	Booth W. Kelly Ltd, Ramsey (S)

Mary Pullman on display on the RNLI's stand at the Earls Court Boat Show in London, 9 January 1965. (Jeff Morris)

Mary Pullman on display in the Bull Ring Shopping Centre, Birmingham, 22 April 1965, prior to going on station at Kirkcudbright. (Jeff Morris)

7.9.1985 – 7.12.1985	Kirkcudbright (sl)
8.12.1985 – 22.2.1986	Workington (temp relief)
22.2.1986 – 29.5.1986	Herd & Mackenzie, Buckie (S, I)
29.5.1986 – 3.6.1986	Passage to Kirkcudbright (via Caledonian Canal, Oban, Islay, Portpatrick)
3.6.1986 – 24.4.1989	Kirkcudbright (sl)
24.4.1989 – 25.4.1989	Passage to Silver Marine, Rosneath (via Girvan)
25.4.1989 – 1.8.1990	Silver Marine, Rosneath (S and I, found to be beyond economic repair so withdrawn, and Kirkcudbright became an Atlantic station from 3.5.1989)

Notable Rescues

During her time at Kirkcudbright, *Mary Pullman* was involved in two notable rescues. The first took place on 17 May 1976 when she was launched in a southerly gale force eight and very rough seas to two persons who were reported to be stranded on a rock at the mouth of the River Dee. Under the command of Coxswain George Davidson, the lifeboat headed across the bay in very rough seas, frequently disappearing from the sight of people watching from the shore. Just over ten minutes after launching, the lifeboat reached Frenchman's Rock, about one mile west of the lifeboat house, and found two men in great danger of being washed off the rock.

The lifeboat was anchored 30m to the south of the rock and the lifeboatmen fired a rocket line over the heads of the two men to the Coast Rescue Equipment company who had mustered on the far shore. The wind was still gale force eight and Coxswain Davidson had continuously to use the lifeboat's engines and adjust the cable to keep the veering line within reach of the survivors. The two men were then taken off the rock by breeches buoy, with one suffering from hypothermia. Once on board the lifeboat both were wrapped in blankets and the coxswain radioed for a doctor to be waiting. At about 2.50 p.m. the two men were landed at the harbour where the lifeboat stayed until conditions on the slipway improved.

For this rescue, the Thanks on Vellum was accorded to Coxswain/Mechanic George Davidson and Vellum service certificates were presented to the remainder of the crew: Second Coxswain James Little, Assistant Mechanic William McKie and crew members Edward Eccles, Stephen Eccles, Colin Mathieson, Charles Devlin and Alexander McHenry.

The crew of *Mary Pullman* performed another Vellum service on 26 November 1984. At 10.05 p.m. the lifeboat was launched to the fishing vessel *Leon Jeannine*, of Brixham, which was stranded on Kirkcudbright bar and required immediate assistance. With Acting Coxswain/Mechanic Stephen Unsworth in command, a sharp visual and radar watch was set as the vessel was reported to be in Kirkcudbright channel.

Five minutes after launching, the lifeboat cleared the bar, having sighted nothing. As the coxswain headed west, two minutes later the casualty was spotted, stranded and lying on her starboard side in breaking seas. Three people were on board and they were instructed to move to the stern of the vessel. As the lifeboat passed the stern of the casualty, the three froze and would not leave the wreck.

A second run was made and this time the crew on the lifeboat's foredeck grabbed a survivor each and pulled him aboard. The lifeboat then headed south to clear the bank before turning to cross the bar and return to her station. Just over half an hour after launching, the lifeboat was back on the slipway and the three survivors had been landed.

For this rescue, the Thanks on Vellum was accorded to Acting Coxswain/ Mechanic Unsworth, while Vellum service certificates were presented to the rest of the crew.

Mary Pullman on the slipway at Kirkcudbright on 26 July 1988. (Tony Denton)

The dramatic sight of *Mary Pullman* launching down the slipway at Kirkcudbright for a routine exercise on 26 July 1988. (Tony Denton)

Disposal

After a survey and inspection at Silver Marine, Rosneath, between 25 April 1989 and 1 March 1990 revealed considerable deterioration of her hull, *Mary Pullman* was declared non-operational on 1 January 1991 as it was deemed imprudent to carry out necessary repairs. Originally she was allocated for display at the International Boatbuilding Training Centre (IBTC), Oulton Broad, Lowestoft, but instead a decision was made to scrap her. However, although the Director of the IBTC reported on 9 June 1992 that she had been broken in two parts through the aft end of the forward cockpit, she remains intact and is now on display outside the Baytree Garden Centre, High Road, Weston, near Spalding, Lincolnshire.

Ernest Tom Neathercoat

Official Number	982
Operational Number	37-15
Year built	1965
Builder	William Osborne, Littlehampton
Yard No.	WO 982
Cost	£34,000
Donor	Provided from a legacy left by Mr E.T. Neathercoat, CBE, of Horsham, Sussex and the general funds of the RNLI.
Named	8 July 1965 by HRH Princess Marina, Duchess of Kent at Wells.

Stations

| Wells | June 1965 – July 1990 | 85/16 |
| North Sunderland | Aug. 1990 – July 1991 | 16/0 |

Movements

1.6.1965 – 7.12.1982	Wells (sl)
7.12.1982 – 23.7.1983	Brown's Bt Yd, Rowhedge (S)
23.7.1983 – 24.7.1983	Passage to Wells
24.7.1983 – 28.11.1986	Wells (sl)
28.11.1986 – 1.12.1986	Passage to Crescent Marine
1.12.1986 – 12.4.1988	Crescent Marine, Otterham Quay (S)
12.4.1988 – 14.4.1988	Passage to Wells
14.4.1988 – 15.5.1990	Wells (sl)
15.5.1990 – 6.7.1990	Wells (relief at Wells, new lifeboat ON.1161 placed on service 3.7.1990)
6.7.1990 – 9.8.1990	Leggett's Bt Yd, Grimsby (I)
9.8.1990 – 14.8.1990	Marshall Branson Ltd, Amble
14.8.1990 – 15.8.1990	Passage to North Sunderland
15.8.1990 – 8.8.1991	North Sunderland (TSD)
8.8.1991 – 25.11.1991	Marshall Branson Ltd, Amble (ER and std)
25.11.1991	Passage to RNLI Depot, Poole
25.11.1991 – 12.2.1992	RNLI Depot, Poole (ER)
12.2.1992 – 28.4.1992	RNLI Depot, Poole (std)

Ernest Tom Neathercoat in her early days as Wells' lifeboat.

Ernest Tom Neathercoat being recovered on the beach at Wells in front of the lifeboat house. (Paul Russell)

Notable Rescues

During her time at Wells, *Ernest Tom Neathercoat* was involved in two very long and arduous services that tested her crew to the very limit of their endurance. The first took place on 15 February 1979 when she was launched to the Romanian cargo vessel *Savinesti*, with twenty-eight people on board, which had broken down in violent winds, gusting to hurricane force, with a continuous blizzard and very rough seas. The lifeboat was launched into Wells harbour under the command of Coxswain David Cox and was immediately confronted by heavy rolling seas which continually filled her cockpits, and put her radar and echo sounder out of action.

Bridlington and Humber lifeboats were also launched to assist the cargo vessel. The 54ft Arun *City of Bradford IV* (ON.1052) left the Humber in a blizzard, and with a temperature of minus four degrees centigrade there was a 3in layer of ice on the boat and its rails. The radar scanners were coated in thick ice which had to be chipped away before the lifeboat could continue passage.

At 12.13 p.m., the crew of *Ernest Tom Neathercoat* sighted the casualty and soon began standing by. At 1.14 p.m. Coxswain Cox asked if he could be relieved by the Humber Arun as soon as possible because his crew were extremely cold. For the next two hours, however, the open lifeboat stood by the casualty in temperatures well below freezing, washed by huge waves, until the Humber lifeboat arrived at 3.00 p.m.

The return passage was made at half speed with the drogue streamed and snow blowing directly into the aft cockpit. The wind was storm force eleven gusting to hurricane force twelve with snow blowing directly into the aft cockpit. At 6.15 p.m.

shore lights were spotted, so a parachute flare was put up and the coastguard confirmed the lifeboat's position as being just north of Brancaster Golf Course. An easterly course was then set for Wells, but the remaining seven miles took two hours.

At 8.26 p.m. the lifeboat was just west of Wells Bar and at 9.10 p.m. the lifeboat crossed the bar, guided by a local fishing boat. The lifeboat berthed in the harbour at 9.50 p.m. The crew were all helped ashore and most found that they were unable to walk. They were helped into a change of clothes and driven to their homes.

In all, *Ernest Tom Neathercoat* had been at sea for eleven hours and twenty-four minutes in violent storm conditions with heavy swells and phenomenal seas frequently washing right over the lifeboat, a continuous blizzard, poor visibility and sub-zero temperatures. For this extraordinary service, the Silver medal was awarded to Coxswain Cox and Medal Service Certificates were presented to the remainder of the crew, Second Coxswain Anthony Jordan, Mechanic Albert Court, Assistant Mechanic Alan Cox and crew members Albert Warner, John Nudds, Graham Walker and John Betts. The *Savinesti* made the River Humber under her own power escorted by two tugs.

The second of the outstanding rescues performed by the Wells crew in *Ernest Tom Neathercoat* formally recognised by the RNLI took place on 20 November 1981. The lifeboat was launched under the command of Coxswain David Cox after a casualty had been reported north of Brancaster. A force eight gale was blowing and the weather was overcast.

At 3.42 p.m. the casualty, the motor fishing vessel *Sarah K*, was sighted. It had a flooded engine room and was in danger in the heavy seas. At 4.30 p.m. the lifeboat approached the casualty and skipper requested a tow to King's Lynn. However, the casualty was too large to be towed by the lifeboat so Coxswain Cox decided to take the crew off. Four approaches to the casualty were made by the lifeboat in the heavy seas and total darkness to successfully take off the crew of four. The skipper was the last to leave. The lifeboat then returned to her station.

For this rescue, the Bronze medal was awarded to Coxswain Cox; Medal service certificates were presented to the remainder of the crew, Second Coxswain Anthony Jordan, Mechanic Albert Court, Assistant Mechanic Alan Cox and crew members Albert Warner, Graham Walker, John Nudds and John Betts.

Disposal

After her last inspection on 21 August 1990, *Ernest Tom Neathercoat* was stored at the RNLI Depot, Poole, until 28 April 1992. She was then transported overland to the International Boatbuilding Training Centre, Oulton Broad, near Lowestoft. In 1993 she was placed on display outside the Training Centre's buildings at Oulton Broad. In 1998 she was moved to the beach car park at Wells-next-the-Sea, and is now displayed there close to the lifeboat station where she served.

The Doctors

Official Number	983
Operational Number	37–16
Year built	1965
Builder	William Osborne, Littlehampton
Yard No.	WO 983
Cost	£34,000
Donor	Gift of Dr Nora Allan, of Bearsden, Glasgow, in memory of her late father Dr Richard Allan, late of the Ministry of Health, Dumbarton, and of her brothers, Dr John Allan, Dr William Allan, of Greenock, and James Allan.
Named	28 July 1965 by HRH the Duchess of Gloucester, at Anstruther.

Stations
Anstruther	26 May 1965 – Aug. 1991	78*/22
Relief	1991 – 1993	0/0

*including one service carried out while on passage.

Movements
26.5.1965 – 4.2.1979	Anstruther (sl)
4.2.1979 – 19.5.1979	Coastal Marine, Eyemouth (rlvd by ON.942)
19.5.1979 – 17.7.1984	Anstruther (sl)
17.7.1984 – 19.7.1984	Passage to Herd & Mackenzie Bt Yd
19.7.1984 – 23.2.1985	Herd & Mackenzie Bt Yd, Buckie (S, rlvd by ON. 984)
23.2.1985 – 25.2.1985	Passage to Anstruther
25.2.1985 – 5.5.1987	Anstruther (sl)
5.5.1987 – 6.5.1987	Passage to Herd & Mackenzie Bt Yd, Buckie
6.5.1987 – 22.7.1988	Herd & Mackenzie Bt Yd, Buckie (S, rlvd by ON.975)
22.7.1988 – 24.7.1988	Passage to Anstruther
24.7.1988 – 15.5.1990	Anstruther (sl)

The Doctors in her early days at Anstruther. (From a postcard supplied by David Gooch)

Above: The Doctors heads out of Anstruther Harbour. (W.F. Flett). *Below:* Launching *The Doctors* for Anstruther's annual Lifeboat Day in August 1981. (Tony Denton)

15.3.1991 – 17.3.1991   Passage to Buckie (via Stonehaven 15.3.91,
                          Fraserburgh 16.3.91)
17.3.1991 – 11.7.1992   Jones' Bt Yd, Buckie (ER)
11.7.1992 – 10.5.1993   Jones' Bt Yd, Buckie (std)

Notable Rescues

On 31 January 1980, *The Doctors* was launched at 5.26 a.m. under the command of
Coxswain Peter Murray to the fishery cruiser *Switha*, a 573-ton ex-research trawler
built in 1948, which was hard aground and holed on the Herwit Rock, about a mile
south-east of Inchkeith Island. The lifeboat reached the casualty at 7.33 a.m., having
fought her way through a force nine gale and very rough seas.

By this time, the *Switha*'s master had agreed for non-essential crew to be airlifted
ashore by helicopter. The lifeboat was therefore required to stand by and provide
surface support for the helicopter when necessary. After more than five hours, one
lifeboatman began to suffer from exhaustion and cold so he was landed at Leith. The
lifeboat returned to the vessel and remained on stand by until after 4.00 p.m.,
returning to station after almost eleven hours at sea in freezing conditions.

For this service, a Letter of Thanks signed by the Chief of Operations was sent to
the Honorary Secretary in recognition of the efforts of the coxswain and crew to help
the cruiser.

Disposal

The Doctors was taken to Buckie in March 1991, and kept at Jones' Boat Yard from
17 March 1991 until being declared non-operational on 11 July 1993 when she was
placed on the sale list. She was sold to Moray District Council in 1993 and was subsequently exhibited outside the Drifter Centre, Buckie, as part of a display at the
Centre relating to the lifeboat service.

Mary Joicey

Official Number	984
Operational Number	37–17
Year built	1964
Builder	Herd & MacKenzie, Buckie
Yard No.	–
Cost	£37,000
Donor	Donation from the trustees of the late Mrs Mary Joicey, Sunningdale, Berks, and RNLI General Funds.
Named	10 June 1967 by the Viscountess Ridley, of Blagdon at Newbiggin.

Stations

Newbiggin	Sept. 1966 – Mar. 1981	52/24
Relief	1981 – 1989	52/12
Redcar	July 1985 – Mar. 1986	2/0

Movements

5.9.1966 – 15.7.1971	Newbiggin (sl)
15.7.1971 – 15.11.1971	Boatyard (S, Oh, rlvd by ON.979)
15.11.1971 – 15.7.1977	Newbiggin (sl)
15.7.1977 – 1.3.1978	Boatyard (S, Oh, rlvd by ON.979)
1.3.1978 – 26.2.1981	Newbiggin (sl, withdrawn 28.2.1981, Newbiggin became Atlantic station)
26.2.1981 – 15.4.1981	Harrison Bt Yd, Amble (S, allocated to relief fleet)
15.4.1981 – 5.6.1981	Redcar (rlvg ON.975: 0/0)
5.6.1981 – 30.9.1981	Bridlington (rlvg ON.980: 4/0)
30.9.1981 – 27.3.1982	Dungeness (rlvg ON.1048: 6/2)
27.3.1982 – 1.4.1982	Passage to Amble (via Ramsgate, Lowestoft, Wells, Bridlington and Hartlepool)
1.4.1982 – 23.7.1982	Harrison Bt Yd, Amble (S)
23.7.1982 – 19.3.1983	Filey (rlvg ON.966: 5/1)
19.3.1983 – 18.12.1983	Scarborough (rlvg ON.979: 8/0)
18.12.1983 – 7.1.1984	Dickie's Bt Yd, Bangor (Ovh, I)
7.1.1984 – 9.7.1984	Port Erin (rlvg ON.998: 0/0)
9.7.1984 – 14.7.1984	Holyhead Bt Yd (I)
14.7.1984 – 15.7.1984	Passage to Anstruther (via Robson's Bt Yd, South Shields, and Eyemouth)
15.7.1984 – 26.2.1985	Anstruther (rlvg ON.983)
26.2.1985 – 13.7.1985	Nth Sunderland (rlvg ON.991: 6/6)
13.7.1985 – 24.3.1986	Redcar (rlvg: 2/0)
24.3.1986 – 5.10.1986	Harrison Bt Yd, Amble (S, fitted with folding wh over cockpit)
5.10.1986 – 6.10.1986	Passage to Skegness (via Whitby)
6.10.1986 – 28.3.1988	Skegness (rlvg ON.977: 7/0)
28.3.1988 – 29.3.1988	Passage to Woodbridge (via Lowestoft)
29.3.1988 – 12.5.1988	Whisstocks Bt Yd, Woodbridge (R, S and I)
12.5.198 – 13.5.1988	Passage to Hastings (via Ramsgate)
13.5.1988 – 15.3.1989	Hastings (rlvg ON.973: 9/0)
15.3.1989 – 17.3.1989	Passage to St Ives (via Littlehampton, Poole, Brixham and Falmouth)
17.3.1989 – 24.3.1989	Fairey Marine Ltd, Cowes (HR; while on passage from Hastings to St Ives leaks found in hull, so diverted to Fairey Marine for R)
24.3.1989 – 27.3.1989	RNLI Depot, Poole (std)
27.3.1989 – 29.3.1989	Passage to St Ives (via Brixham and Falmouth)
29.3.1989 – 22.9.1989	St Ives (TSD: 5/0)
22.9.1989 – 25.9.1989	Passage to RNLI Depot, Poole
25.9.1989 – 28.11.1989	RNLI Depot, Poole (I, std)

Mary Joicey on the beach at Newbiggin in July 1980. (Richard Martin)

Notable Rescues

While in service at Newbiggin, *Mary Joicey* was involved in two notable rescues. On 31 January 1975 she was launched after a rowing boat, with two fishermen on board, had capsized in a rough sea. A coble, *Margaret Lisle*, was also launched to assist. By the time the lifeboat arrived on the scene, the capsized boat had been carried further out by the tide and was some 150yds offshore. The coble then reached the casualty, by which time there was only one person still holding onto the capsized boat.

Because of the motion of the breaking seas the lifeboat circled the casualty and the coble's crew recovered the survivor, who had been in the water for twenty minutes and was exhausted. During the operation, the lifeboat was continually swept by breaking seas. After the coble had landed the survivor, the lifeboat continued to search for the other man. Although he was found quite soon, and was winched from the lifeboat to be taken direct to Ashington hospital, he failed to respond to treatment and died.

For this rescue, the Thanks on Vellum was accorded to both Acting Coxswain George Dawson and the skipper of the coble, John Robinson; Vellum service certificates were presented to the remainder of the crews of both the coble and the lifeboat.

Almost nineteen months after this rescue, *Mary Joicey* was involved in another service which earned recognition for her crew. On Sunday 29 August 1976, two swimmers were swept out to sea from Cambois; a girl bather had been picked up by a helicopter, but her father was missing. Both the Blyth D class inshore lifeboat and *Mary Joicey*, from Newbiggin, under the command of Coxswain George Dawson, were launched to search for the missing man. Unfortunately, after more than an hour

Mary Joicey on relief duty at Bridlington, launching for the station's Lifeboat Day in August 1983. (Nicholas Leach)

nothing had been found either inshore where the ILB was searching, or offshore, where *Mary Joicey* was operating.

A further call for assistance then came from the Coastguard after the cabin cruiser *Janpaumar* had been reported capsized off the mouth of the River Wansbeck, and so both lifeboats were diverted to this incident. The ILB arrived first, assessed the situation and, once *Mary Joicey* had arrived, it was decided to tow the casualty clear. Two attempts were made to transfer a line to the cabin cruiser, which was being pounded by the heavy surf, but neither was successful. At this time the ILB was swamped by a large wave, her engine could not be restarted, and *Mary Joicey* had to tow her clear of the surf.

Coxswain Dawson then took *Mary Joicey* towards the cabin cruiser. At the second attempt a line was passed to the casualty, her crew secured it and the lifeboat then towed the vessel clear of the surf line into calmer water. Taking the ILB in tow as well, *Mary Joicey* then headed for Blyth and arrived in the harbour without further incident.

For this rescue, the Thanks on Vellum was accorded to both Coxswain Dawson and the helmsman of Blyth's ILB, David Tilmouth. Vellum service certificates were presented to the crewmembers from both lifeboats involved in this service.

Disposal

Mary Joicey was placed on the sale list on 1 November 1989, and left the RNLI Depot, Poole, on 28 November. She was loaned to the Child-Beale Wildlife Trust, Reading, Berkshire, where she was placed on display.

Valentine Wyndham-Quin

Official Number	985
Operational Number	37-18
Year built	1967
Builder	Herd & MacKenzie, Buckie
Yard No.	–
Cost	£37,000
Donor	Legacy of Mr H.P. Harris, Dorridge, an anonymous gift and RNLI funds.
Named	24 April 1968 by HRH Princess Marina, at Clacton-on-Sea.

Stations

Clacton-on-Sea	Jan. 1968 – July 1983	184/61
Clogher Head	Aug. 1984 – Sept. 1988	9/5

Movements

19.1.1968 – 8.5.1976	Clacton-on-Sea (sl)
8.5.1976 – 13.11.1976	Boatyard (S, Ovh, rlvd by ON.961)
13.11.1976 – 31.1.1978	Clacton-on-Sea (sl)
31.1.1978 – 8.3.1978	Cardnell Bt Yd, Maylandsea (S, rlvd by ON.922)
8.3.1978 – 9.8.1980	Clacton-on-Sea (sl)
9.8.1980 – 14.3.1981	Brown's Bt Yd, Rowhedge (S and I)
14.3.1981 – 12.7.1983	Clacton-on-Sea (sl)
12.7.1983 – 30.6.1984	Crescent Marine, Otterham Quay (S, rlvg ON.934)
30.6.1984 – 2.7.1984	Clacton-on-Sea (sl)

Valentine Wyndham-Quin puts to sea after her naming ceremony in April 1968. (Jeff Morris)

Valentine Wyndham-Quin with engine casing painted orange. (From a postcard supplied by Mark Roberts)

2.7.1984 – 5.7.1984	Crescent Marine, Otterham Quay (awaiting passage)
5.7.1984 – 7.7.1984	Passage to RNLI Depot, Poole (via Ramsgate and Newhaven)
7.7.1984 – 14.7.1984	RNLI Depot, Poole (std)
14.7.1984 – 19.7.1984	Passage to Clogher Head (via Brixham, Newlyn, Rosslare, Howth)
19.7.1984 – 23.8.1984	Bangor Bt Yd, Northern Ireland
23.8.1984 – 2.3.1985	Clogher Head (sl)
2.3.1985 – 17.4.1985	Tyrrells Bt Yd, Arklow (R)
17.4.1985 – 23.5.1988	Clogher Head (sl, withdrawn 23.5.1988, station temporarily closed)
23.5.1988 – 22.11.1988	Tyrrells Bt Yd, Arklow (S)

Notable Rescues

On 20 November 1971 red flares were sighted in the area of the Wallet Spitway buoy off Clacton-on-Sea and so, at 6.17 p.m., *Valentine Wyndham-Quin* was launched under the command of Coxswain Charles Bolingbroke. The lifeboat started searching the area where the flares had been reported in wind which was force five to six with rain squalls.

By 7.11 p.m. the wind had increased to force seven and force eight to nine was forecast. At 7.58 p.m. the lifeboat started searching near the West Swinn buoy and ten minutes later spotted the casualty, *Zona*, an old pilot boat, in tow of the cabin cruiser *Pisces* close to the West Barrow Sands. Coxswain Bolingbroke approached *Zona* in only 5-6ft of water, and managed to take off her two crew at the first approach despite the short, steep seas. The lifeboat then took off the cabin cruiser's crew without injury to anyone or damage to the boat.

On the return journey the wind was force eight to nine, gusting to ten, with very rough seas and visibility near zero in heavy rain. The lifeboat reached Brightlingsea after 11.00 p.m. where all the survivors were landed. For this rescue, in which five people had been saved in the space of twenty minutes, the Thanks on Vellum was accorded to Coxswain Bolingbroke; Letters of Appreciation signed by the Chairman of the Institution, Admiral Sir Wilfred Wood, were sent to the rest of the crew.

On 15 July 1974 *Valentine Wyndham-Quin* was involved in another notable rescue. She was launched shortly after 4.30 p.m. in a force seven to gale force eight wind, with rough seas. At 7.25 p.m. the lifeboat sighted the casualty, the motor barge *Minnie Ha Ha*, aground in breaking seas on the Middle Sunk Sands. Her main engine and steering had broken down and her crew were sailing for the Thames Estuary to seek shelter.

In order to approach the casualty the lifeboat had to navigate very shallow waters, but when she was close enough a line was passed to the barge. A tow was attempted but the lines parted as the violent motion of the barge in the deeper water created too great a strain on the line.

At 8.10 p.m. the survey vessel HMS *Echo* arrived on the scene and a heavier tow-line was rigged. The casualty was then towed westward towards the shelter of the River Crouch. The lifeboat stood by until the tow reached the Whitaker Channel and then made for Brightlingsea, as re-housing at Clacton would have been impossible in the conditions.

For this rescue, the Thanks on Vellum was accorded to Coxswain Bolingbroke; Vellum certificates were presented to the remainder of the crew, Second Coxswain Arthur Harman, Acting Mechanic Jack Bolingbroke and crew members David Wells, Philip Sherman, Bernard Drane and Robert Smith.

Disposal

After survey at Arklow it was decided, in November 1988, that *Valentine Wyndham-Quin* was fit only for display and should not be sold. She was sailed to Holyhead Boat Co. on 22 November 1988, lifted out of the water and has not been refloated since. She was placed on display outside the Lifeboat Museum at Cromer, and has subsequently been moved to Harwich for display inside the Lifeboat Museum.

Valentine Wyndham-Quin at Clogher Head. (Colin Watson)

Lloyd's II

Official Number   986
Operational Number   37-19
Year built   1966
Builder   Morris & Lorimer, Sandbank
Yard No.   –
Cost   £34,000
Donor   Gift from the Corporation of Lloyd's and Lloyd's
                           Brokers.
Named   Ilfracombe on 13 September 1966 by Mrs Sturge, wife
                           of the Chairman of Lloyd's, at Ilfracombe.

Stations

Ilfracombe   July 1966 – June 1990   136/116
Sheringham   Oct. 1990 – Apr. 1992   12/0

Movements

8.7.1966 – 2.7.1976   Ilfracombe (sl)
2.7.1976 – 14.12.1976   Boatyard (S, Ovh, radar installed, rlvd by ON.974)
14.12.1976 – 26.4.1981   Ilfracombe (sl)
26.4.1981 – 27.4.1981   Passage to Falmouth
27.4.1981 – 19.10.1981   Falmouth Bt Co., Falmouth (rlvd by ON.994)
19.10.1981 – 20.10.1981   Passage to Ilfracombe

Lloyds II being recovered on the beach in the outer harbour at Ilfracombe. (From an old postcard supplied by David Gooch)

Lloyds II outside the lifeboat house at Ilfracombe. (Phil Weeks)

20.10.1981 – 22.4.1985	Ilfracombe (sl)
22.4.1985 – 24.4.1985	Passage to Falmouth
24.4.1985 – 29.6.1985	Falmouth Bt Co., Falmouth (S, rlvd by ON.942)
29.6.1985 – 1.7.1985	Passage to Ilfracombe
1.7.1985 – 3.12.1986	Ilfracombe (sl)
3.12.1986 – 4.12.1986	Appledore Sh Yd, North Devon
4.12.1986 – 5.12.1986	Passage to Cowes (via Berthon Bt Co., Lymington)
5.12.1986 – 30.10.1987	Fairey Marine Ltd, Cowes (HR, rlvd by ON.1047)
30.10.1987 – 1.11.1987	Passage to Ilfracombe
1.11.1987 – 9.11.1987	St Ives (T)
9.11.1987 – 10.11.1987	Passage to Cowes (via Plymouth 9.11.87 and Weymouth 10.11.87)
10.11.1987 – 2.12.1987	Fairey Marine Ltd, Cowes (T)
2.12.1987 – 5.12.1987	Passage to Ilfracombe
5.12.1987 – 16.5.1990	Ilfracombe (sl)
16.5.1990 – 25.7.1990	Ilfracombe (awaiting departure, new lifeboat ON.1165 at Ilfracombe)
25.7.1990 – 4.10.1990	Marine Port Services, Pembroke Dock (ER)
4.10.1990 – 7.10.1990	Passage overland to Lowestoft.
7.10.1990★ – 8.10.1990	Passage Lowestoft to Sheringham (via Gorleston)
8.10.1990 – 18.4.1992	Sheringham (TSD, Sheringham became Atlantic station)
18.4.1992 – 24.4.1992	Fletcher's Bt Yd, Lowestoft (last I 22.9.1990)
24.4.1992 – 29.4.1992	Passage overland to Otterham Quay
29.4.1992 – 30.8.1993	Crescent Marine, Otterham Quay (std, ER)

★While on passage on 7.10.1990, *Lloyds II*, along with the Gorleston inshore lifeboat, went to the assistance of the yacht *Lady of Thane*, which had broken down at the entrance to Great Yarmouth harbour. Following this service, *Lloyds II* continued her passage to Sheringham.

Notable Rescue

On 9 September 1984, *Lloyds II* was launched under the command of Coxswain David Clemence to the yacht *Liberty*, which was in imminent danger of being driven on to rocks near Ilfracombe harbour. One of the two men on board had radioed that his skipper appeared to be dead and he had no experience of boats. The wind was north-westerly force seven, gusting to gale force eight, and a very rough sea was running.

The lifeboat reached the yacht shortly after launching and found her dragging her anchor rapidly towards Rappraree Beach. In only about 10ft of water, she was touching the bottom in the trough of each wave. It was impossible to get alongside, but Coxswain Clemence took the lifeboat to within 10ft of her, enabling the lifeboat crew to pass a line to the man on board the casualty.

Once the line was secured, the lifeboat pulled the yacht clear of the rocks. Because the rough seas still prevented the coxswain putting a man aboard the yacht, it was decided to tow her back into harbour. Turning the lifeboat with the yacht in tow was a difficult manoeuvre, and both lifeboat and yacht endured violent rolling in the seas, which were now beam on. When only 200yds from the harbour, the lifeboat twice rolled heavily to port onto her beam ends in the breaking seas. Throughout the tow a crew member was at the lifeboat's stern with an axe, ready to part the tow rope should it become necessary. Fortunately, the two boats safely reached the relative calm of the outer harbour. The lifeboat then went alongside the casualty, a lifeboatman was put aboard, and both boats were taken into the inner harbour. The waiting ambulancemen reported that the skipper of the yacht was dead but one crew member from the yacht had been saved.

For this rescue, the Bronze medal was awarded to Coxswain Clemence; Medal service certificates were presented to the rest of the crew, Second Coxswain Colin Thadwald, Mechanic Wayland Smith, Assistant Mechanic John Fennell and crew Andrew Bengey, David P. Clemence and Maurice Woodiger.

Disposal

Lloyd's II was broken up at Crescent Marine, Otterham Quay, December 1993.

Edward and Mary Lester

Official Number	991
Operational Number	37-20
Year built	1967
Builder	William Osborne, Littlehampton
Yard No.	WO 991
Cost	£37,500
Donor	Gift and legacy of the late Mrs Mary Lester, of Caernarvon.
Named	16 September 1967 by Lady Victoria Percy, daughter of the Duke and Duchess of Northumberland at Seahouses harbour.

Edward and Mary Lester on display to the public in the harbour during North Sunderland's Lifeboat Day at Seahouses harbour. (Tony Denton)

Edward and Mary Lester approaching Seahouses harbour during Lifeboat Day. (Tony Denton)

Stations

| North Sunderland | July 1967 – Mar. 1989 | 109/27 |

Movements

18.7.1967 – 28.8.1976	North Sunderland (sl)
28.8.1976 – 19.10.1976	Survey (rlvd by ON.979)
19.10.1976 – 4.8.1980	North Sunderland (sl)
4.8.1980 – 14.11.1980	Harrison Bt Yd, Amble (S, rlvd by ON.972)
14.11.1980 – 27.2.1985	North Sunderland (sl)

Edward and Mary Lester moored in the harbour at Seahouses during Lifeboat Day. (Tony Denton)

27.2.1985 – 12.7.1985	Harrison Bt Yd, Amble (S, rlvd by ON.984)
12.7.1985 – 31.3.1989	North Sunderland (sl)
31.3.1989 – 26.4.1989	Robson's Bt Yd, South Shields (S, rlvd by ON.980)
26.4.1989 – 1.10.1989	RNLI Depot, Poole (std)

Notable Rescues

Although *Edward and Mary Lester* did not perform any service for which awards to her crew were made, she frequently went to the aid of fishing vessels. The following is typical of the kind of service she often performed while stationed at North Sunderland.

On 10 September 1972, the fishing vessel *Constance* ran aground on the Knavestone Rock. Her crew called for help, and *Edward and Mary Lester* launched at 10.40 p.m. but, because it was low tide, was unable to get close to the stranded vessel.

To contact the casualty, a rocket line was fired to the three fishermen on board the stranded coble. The fishermen got into a life raft to which they tied the rocket. The life raft was then hauled to the lifeboat and the fishermen were taken on board. The lifeboat continued to stand by the stranded vessel until, on the rising tide, she refloated. However, she had been badly damaged by the rocks and sank almost immediately.

Disposal

Following a survey at Robson's Boat Yard, South Shields, *Edward and Mary Lester* was withdrawn from service at North Sunderland. She was stored at the RNLI Depot, Poole, then dismantled and broken up at Belsize Bt Yd, 44 Priory Road, St Denys, Southampton, in October 1989.

Frank Penfold Marshall

Official Number	992
Operational Number	37–21
Year built	1968
Builder	William Osborne, Littlehampton
Yard No.	WO 992
Cost	£38,207
Donor	Gift of Mrs Dagmar Marshall in memory of her husband, the late Lt-Col. Frank Penfold Marshall OBE.
Named	12 June 1969 by Mrs Dagmar Marshall at St Ives.

Stations

St Ives   July 1968 – March 1989   227*/85
*Including one service carried out while on passage.

Frank Penfold Marshall being recovered on the beach at St Ives during her early years of service, with her engine casing painted grey. (David Gooch)

Frank Penfold Marshall off St Ives after the aft cockpit had been enclosed and radar had been fitted. (From a postcard in the author's collection)

Frank Penfold Marshall seen from the air. (RNAS Culdrose, by courtesy of the RNLI)

Movements

6.7.1968 – 27.10.1978	St Ives (sl; first 37ft Oakley to be fitted with radar)
12.7.1970 – 5.4.1971	Survey (rlvd by ON.994)
5.4.1971 – 2.1.1975	St Ives (sl)
2.1.1975 – 2.7.1976★	Survey (rlvd by ON.974)
2.7.1976 – 27.10.1978	St Ives (sl)
27.10.1978 – 4.5.1979	Falmouth Bt Co., Falmouth (HR, rlvd by ON.961)
4.5.1979 – 27.6.1983	St Ives (sl)
27.6.1983 – 29.6.1983	Passage to RNLI Depot, Poole (rlvd by ON. 994)
29.6.1983 – 20.4.1984	Branksea Marine, Wareham (S and R, rlvd by ON.994)
20.4.1984 – 23.4.1984	Passage to St Ives
23.4.1984 – 13.3.1989	St Ives (sl)
13.3.1989 – 16.3.1989	St Ives (rlvd by ON.984 at St Ives)
16.3.1989 – 26.4.1989	Falmouth Bt Co., Falmouth (R, ON.984 at St Ives on TSD from 29.3.1989)
26.4.1989 – 1.10.1989	RNLI Depot, Poole (std)

★On 6 June 1976, during a passage from Newhaven to Dover, she gave help to the fishing vessel *Florence Haffly*.

Notable Rescues

In the early hours of 24 December 1977, *Frank Penfold Marshall* was launched from St Ives to the Danish coaster *Lady Kamilla* which was in distress twenty miles due north of St Ives in a west-south-westerly storm and a very heavy sea. Together with lifeboats from Padstow and Clovelly, as well as various helicopters and other vessels in the area, the St Ives lifeboat assisted in a prolonged search for the coaster's crew, who had abandoned ship.

During this search, which was undertaken in strong gale force winds and an exceptionally high sea, the lifeboat was nearly capsized after being hit by a very large sea. She heeled over to an angle of 90 degrees and was submerged by the enormous wave that had hit her. None of the lifeboat crew were washed overboard, and the coxswain was able to continue with the search.

Despite sustaining damage to some of the electronic equipment on board, *Frank Penfold Marshall* continued searching off Porthtowan until 6.30 a.m., when the search was called off. In view of the damage sustained to the boat she was recalled to station, having been at sea for over six hours in appalling conditions. She entered St Ives harbour at 7.00 a.m. and was re-carriaged. Two survivors from the coaster were subsequently picked up from a life raft by helicopter, but no other survivors were found.

For this rescue, the Silver medal was awarded to Coxswain Thomas Cocking in recognition of his courage and seamanship; the Thanks on Vellum was accorded to the remainder of the crew, Second Coxswain John Perkin, Mechanic Philip Penberthy, Assistant Mechanic David Smith, Emergency Mechanic John Thomas, Signalman Eric Ward and Radio Operator Thomas Cocking, Jnr.

Disposal

Following a long service in storm conditions on 12 March 1989, *Frank Penfold Marshall* was placed off service with hull leaks the following day. The lifeboat was taken to the RNLI Depot, Poole, for storage, and then dismantled and broken up at Belsize Boat Yard, St Denys, Southampton, in October 1989.

Frank Penfold Marshall being prepared for a launch at St Ives. (Tony Smith)

Har-Lil

Official Number	993
Operational Number	37-22
Year built	1968
Builder	William Osborne, Littlehampton
Yard No.	WO 993
Cost	£37,000
Donor	Legacy of Miss Jeanie B. Watt, Newton Mearns, Renfrewshire; the boat was named after her late parents, Harry and Lilian.
Named	4 July 1969 by Lady Woods, wife of the RNLI Chairman, at Rhyl.

Stations

Rhyl	Apr. 1968 – Dec. 1990	109/28

Movements

20.4.1968 – 4.3.1979	Rhyl (sl)
4.3.1979 – 14.10.1979	Dickie's Bt Yd, Bangor (S, rlvd by ON.994)
14.10.1979 – 27.10.1979	Extended passage (T at Rhyl)
27.10.1979 – 7.8.1985	Rhyl (sl)
7.8.1985 – 18.10.1985	Dickie's Bt Yd, Bangor (S rlvd by ON.942)
18.10.1985 – 8. 12.1985	Rhyl (sl)
8.12.1985 – 9.12.1985	Craned out of water 8.12.1985, transported overland to Cowes

Launch of *Har-Lil* for Rhyl's annual Lifeboat Day on 3 August 1985 using the Talus MB-H tractor. The gently sloping beach at Rhyl means that, at anything but high tide, the lifeboat has to be taken some way out before a depth of water suitable for launching is reached. (Tony Denton)

Recovery of *Har-Lil* on the beach at Rhyl on 3 August 1985. The procedure to recover the lifeboat onto its carriage was a laborious one and involved many helpers. (Tony Denton)

9.12.1985 – 27.9.1986	Fairey Marine Ltd, Cowes (HR, rlvd by ON.994)
27.9.1986 – 3.10.1986	Passage to Cowes (T)
3.10.1986 – 4.10.1986	Fairey Marine Ltd, Cowes (I)
4.10.1986 – 9.10.1986	Passage to Rhyl
9.10.1986 – 15.5.1990	Rhyl (sl)
15.5.1990 – 23.12.1990	Replaced by ON.1000 (remained at Rhyl)
23.12.1990 – 23.12.1990	Passage to Beaumaris
23.12.1990 – 29.11.1991	Anglesey Bt Yd, Beaumaris (std)

Notable Rescues

Most of the Oakleys served at stations where they were launched from an open beach. However, despite the advantages of powerful tractors, getting the boats afloat sometimes proved very difficult in particularly severe weather. After the yacht *Sussex Bowman*, of Liverpool, was reported to be in difficulties a mile north–east of the lifeboat station at Rhyl on 6 August 1985, getting the Oakley lifeboat afloat to go to the yacht's aid was a severe test for all involved.

The waves breaking on the beach were up to 6ft high and in gale force winds the launch proved to be a very difficult one. *Har-Lil* was taken to the water's edge but just as she was about to be launched, two waves hit the boat and tractor in quick succession, filling the tractor's cab. The pumps in the tractor were engaged to clear the water. Then, just as the order came from Coxswain Herbert to release the boat from her carriage, a third large wave hit, twisting the lifeboat sideways onto the tractor. One of the launching ropes fouled the lifeboat's port propeller, and the crew on board were unable to clear it, so the head launcher waded through the surf and, using the axe from the lifeboat, cut the rope free. The lifeboat was then able to get out to sea and headed for the yacht.

Conditions were too bad for the yacht to enter Rhyl harbour, and so two lifeboatmen were put on board. Four attempts were made to get *Har-Lil* alongside for the transfer to be made, but without success. On the fifth try, with the yacht's head to sea, the lifeboat got close enough for the two lifeboatmen to get on board. The lifeboat then escorted the yacht towards Mostyn Docks. However, when off Prestatyn, to the west of Rhyl, the lifeboat's port engine began giving trouble and had to be shut down. She had to continue on one engine and then safely escorted the yacht into Mostyn Docks. Here the lifeboatmen were able to clear a rope that had fouled the port propeller and the lifeboat returned to Rhyl in the afternoon.

Disposal

Har-Lil left Rhyl on 23 December 1990 and was taken to Anglesey Bt Yd, Beaumaris, where she was stored. After inspection, she was placed on the sale list. She was sold on 1 December 1991 for £1,000 to the Marine Life Centre, St David's, and placed on permanent display there on 12 December 1991. She has been kept outside in the open, and has had her equipment removed.

Vincent Nesfield

Official Number	994
Operational Number	37-23
Year built	1968
Builder	William Osborne, Littlehampton
Yard No.	WO 994
Cost	£38,000
Donor	Proceeds of the Joyce Giddens' Fund, and legacies left by the late Mr James Cowls, Porthleven, Cornwall; and Mr Thomas Ringer, Docking, Norfolk.
Named	9 April 1969 by Mr Esmond Knight at Eastbourne.

Stations

Relief	1969 – 1993	98 /39
Kilmore Quay	Sept. 1989 – Jan. 1991	12/3

Movements

1969 – 1.1.1970	Relief Fleet
1.1.1970 – 17.2.1970	Kirkcudbright (rlvd ON.981: 1/0)
17.2.1970 – 12.7.1970	Llandudno (rlvd ON.976: 2/0)
12.7.1970 – 5.4.1971	St Ives (rlvd ON.992: 4/2)
5.4.1971 – 16.12.1971	Ilfracombe (rlvd ON.986: 3/0)
16.12.1971 – 4.1.1972	Appledore Sh Yd (I and ER)
4.1.1972 – 1.7.1973	Port Erin (relief, kept afloat while slipway altered for Rother: 1/0)
1.7.1973 – 1.5.1974	Holyhead Bt Yd (S, ER)
5.5.1974 – 2.12.1974	Llandudno (rlvd ON.976: 4/0)

Vincent Nesfield on display at the Earls Court Boat Show, London, in January 1969. (Jeff Morris)

2.12.1974 – 25.7.1975	Ramsey (rlvd ON.995: 4/0)
25.7.1975 – 24.11.1975	Kirkcudbright (rlvd ON.981: 1/0)
24.11.1975 – 4.3.1976	Holyhead Bt Yd (S, ER)
4.3.1976 – 30.5.1976	New Quay (rlvd ON.996: 0/0)
30.5.1976 – 14.10.1976	Kilmore Quay (rlvd ON.997: 0/0)
14.10.1976 – 27.10.1976	Arklow (rlvd ON.907: 0/0)
27.10.1976 – 4.11.1976	Extended passage to Sheringham
4.11.1976 – 1.8.1977	Sheringham (rlvd ON.960: 4/0)
1.8.1977 – 10.8.1977	Cardnell Bt Yd, Maylandsea (I)
10.8.1977 – 11.8.1977	Passage to Dungeness
11.8.1977 – 18.8.1977	Dungeness (launching trials)
18.8.1977 – 26.11.1977	Hastings (rlvd ON.973: 5/0)
26.11.1977 – 28.11.1977	Passage to Sennen Cove
1.12.1977 – 16.4.1978	Sennen Cove (rlvd ON.999: 3/6)
16.4.1978 – 19.4.1978	Passage to Dickie's Bt Yd, Bangor
19.4.1978 – 7.7.1978	Dickie's Bt Yd, Bangor (S)
7.7.1978 – 4.3.1979	Llandudno (rlvd ON.976: 3/0)
4.3.1979 – 29.10.1979	Rhyl (rlvd ON.993: 2/0)
29.10.1979 – 9.5.1980	Ramsey (rlvd ON.995: 5/0)
9.5.1980 – 24.4.1981	Dickie's Bt Yd, Bangor (S)
24.4.1981 – 25.4.1981	Passage to Ilfracombe
25.4.1981 – 22.10.1981	Ilfracombe (rlvd ON.986: 5/6)
22.10.1981 – 15.5.1982	Sennen Cove (rlvd ON.999: 4/0)
15.5.1982 – 22.5.1982	Passage to Hoylake
22.5.1982 – 14.7.1982	Hoylake (rlvd ON.1000: 0/0)

14.7.1982 – 15.7.1982	Passage to Moelfre
15.7.1982 – 21.11.1982	Moelfre (rlvd ON.1047: 8/5)
21.11.1982 – 19.6.1983	Kilmore Quay (rlvd ON.997: 0/0)
19.6.1983 – 22.6.1983	Tyrrells Bt Yd, Arklow (I)
22.6.1983 – 23.6.1983	Passage to St Ives
23.6.1983 – 24.4.1984	St Ives (rlvd ON.992, 8/14)
24.4.1984 – 25.4.1984	Passage to New Quay (Dyfed)
25.4.1984 – 19.11.1984	New Quay (rlvd ON.996: 1/0)
19.11.1984 – 26.11.1984	Porthdinllaen (ER: 0/0)
26.11.1984 – 23.7.1985	Llandudno (rlvd ON.976: 4/1)
23.7.1985 – 27.7.1985	Dickie's Bt Yd, Bangor (I)
27.7.1985 – 28.7.1985	Passage to Newcastle (Down)
28.7.1985 – 8.3.1986	Newcastle (rlvd ON.974: 2/0)
8.3.1986 – 14.3.1986	Passage to Cowes
14.3.1986 – 8.3.1987	Fairey Marine Ltd, Cowes (HR)
8.3.1987 – 9.3.1987	RNLI Depot, Poole (for passage)
9.3.1987 – 10.3.1987	Passage to Workington, launched 10.3.1987, and sailed to Ramsey
10.3.1987 – 31.10.1987	Ramsey (rlvd ON.995: 8/2)
31.10.1987 – 1.11.1987	Passage to Pwllheli
1.11.1987 – 2.9.1988	Pwllheli (rlvd ON.978: 3/0)
2.9.1988 – 24.9.1988	Dickie's Bt Yd, Bangor (S)
24.9.1988 – 25.9.1988	Passage to Kilmore Quay
25.9.1988 – 26.1.1991	Kilmore Quay (TSD)
26.1.1991 – 2.1.1992	Arklow Marine & Leisure Ltd, Arklow (std)

Notable Rescue

Vincent Nesfield was on relief duty for almost a year at St Ives during 1983 and 1984. During this time, she was involved in two outstanding rescues on the same day. On 3 January 1984 the West German tug *Fairplay X* fouled her propeller in St Ives Bay while trying to pass a towline to the Netherlands coaster *Orca*. The lifeboat was launched to the tug at 5.00 p.m. under the command of Coxswain Thomas Cocking, Snr, while *Orca*'s anchors appeared to be taking hold. Squalls of rain were being driven down by a gale, and the tug could be clearly seen as the lifeboat left the harbour.

In the force eight gale, with 12ft seas, the casualty was pitching and shipping seas. After fendering the lifeboat's starboard side, Coxswain Cocking made an approach to the tug, and two men jumped aboard. The next run had to be abandoned, but a further approach enabled two more men to jump aboard and another was dragged into the well-deck by two lifeboatmen. As a result of the severe motion alongside, the lifeboat's starboard belting was hanging off.

Because of the possibility of the tug capsizing in the high seas with the gale against the tide, Coxswain Cocking advised the tug's captain to abandon ship and at 5.50 p.m. he agreed. The lifeboat then approached the casualty again, and the two remaining men jumped aboard. The lifeboat came astern, cleared the casualty and set off for St Ives at 5.55 p.m. The tug's crew were safely landed at the harbour.

Vincent Nesfield being recovered on the beach at Ramsey. (Brian Grenfell)

At 10.24 p.m. as the lifeboat was being hauled up the slip on her carriage, a message was received that the coaster *Orca* was dragging her anchor again and required assistance. So the lifeboat was re-launched and, at 10.47 p.m., approached the port side of the coaster. Seas were estimated to be 15ft in height and were breaking over the casualty.

At about 11.00 p.m. Coxswain Cocking brought the lifeboat alongside *Orca*'s port side and one man leapt into the forward well to be received by the lifeboat crew. The jump had to be timed correctly to coincide with the wave crests, after which the lifeboat was driven clear. This manoeuvre was repeated four times, with one man being taken off each time.

The lifeboat then lay off the port side of the casualty, while Falmouth Coastguard advised the master to abandon ship and take to the lifeboat. Two further runs were then made by the lifeboat alongside and the remaining two men were successfully taken off. After a very rough passage back to St Ives, the lifeboat was grounded on the bank, in breaking seas, 50yds off Smeaton Pier. The seven rescued seamen were helped ashore and the lifeboat was re-housed. In total, *Vincent Nesfield* had rescued fourteen people from the two vessels. For these rescues, the Silver medal was awarded to Coxswain Cocking, Snr; Medal service certificates were presented to the crew, Second Coxswain John Perkin, Mechanic Thomas Cocking, Jnr, Assistant Mechanic David Smith, and crew Eric Ward, Philip Allen and Andrew Perkin.

Disposal

In January 1992, *Vincent Nesfield* was taken to Arklow and stored at Arklow Marine & Leisure Ltd. After she was found to be uneconomical to repair, she was broken up in 1995.

James Ball Ritchie

Official Number	995
Operational Number	37-24
Year built	1970
Builder	William Osborne, Littlehampton
Yard No.	WO 995
Cost	£38,500
Donor	Gift from Mrs Ann A. Ritchie, Baldrine, Isle of Man, in fulfilment of her late husband's intention to provide the cost of a lifeboat and in his memory.
Named	9 July 1970 at Ramsey by Mrs Ann Ritchie.

Stations

Ramsey IOM	Feb. 1970 – July 1991	144/77

Movements

22.2.1970 – 2.12.1974	Ramsey (sl)
2.12.1974 – 5.1974	Dickie's Bt Yd, Bangor (S, rlvd by ON.942)
5.1975 – 30.10.1979	Ramsey (sl)
30.10.1979 – 6.5.1980	Dickie's Bt Yd, Bangor (S, rlvd by ON.994)
6.5.1980 – 8.5.1980	Passage to Ramsey
8.5.1980 – 5.7.1985	Ramsey (sl)
5.7.1985 – 6.8.1985	Booth W. Kelly Ltd, Ramsey (S, rlvd by ON.942)

James Ball Ritchie on exercise off Ramsey, July 1989. (Tony Denton)

James Ball Ritchie on her carriage outside the lifeboat house at Ramsey. (Phil Weeks)

James Ball Ritchie off Ramsey during the latter years of her service career. (Tony Denton)

6.8.1985 – 29.11.1986	Ramsey (sl)
29.11.1986 – 29.10.1987	Workington (T, rlvd by ON.994)
29.10.1987 – 26.3.1990	Ramsey (sl)
26.3.1990 – 28.3.1990	Workington (launching trials using tractor and carriage)
28.3.1990 – 12.7.1991	Ramsey (sl)
12.7.1991 – 10.8.1991	Ramsey (awaiting passage to Dumbarton)
10.8.1991 – 12.8.1991	Passage to Dumbarton
12.8.1991 – 12.2.1992	McAllisters Bt Yd, Dumbarton (ER, std)
12.2.1992 – 3.9.1992	McAllisters Bt Yd, Dumbarton (std)

Notable Rescues

In May 1986 the Round the Island Yacht Race took place in the Isle of Man. The race ended with severe weather conditions hampering many of the competitors. The gale force ten winds from the south-south-west created confused and heavy seas that tested the yachts and their crews to the limit and beyond. At 10.48 p.m. on 25 May, *James Ball Ritchie* was launched from Ramsey, under the command of Coxswain James Kinnin, into a force eight gale with rough seas as several yachts in difficulty were unable to make Ramsey harbour.

The first yacht to which the lifeboat went was *Airy Fairy*, in difficulties in Ramsey Bay and unable to make way in the strong winds and rough sea conditions. The lifeboat towed the yacht into Ramsey harbour, and was then immediately requested to proceed to another yacht, *Billy Whizz*, which was similarly unable to make way towards Ramsey.

By the time the lifeboat reached the second yacht, which was four miles away from Ramsey, the wind was estimated to be force nine. Passing a tow to the casualty was difficult, due to the high seas, but the lifeboat was manoeuvred close enough for a line to be got across. As the line was thrown across, the yacht was picked up by a large wave and hurled towards the lifeboat. The yacht struck the lifeboat, narrowly missing the lifeboat's crew, who still managed to pass the towline. Once the tow was secure, the lifeboat made for Ramsey. The force of the seas through which she went slowed the passage considerably, but the harbour was eventually reached and *Billy Whizz* was made secure.

The Honorary Secretary then informed Coxswain Kinnin that another yacht, *Broadaxe*, was in difficulties. Once again *James Ball Ritchie* went out and, with wind and tide behind her, rapidly reached the yacht. The lifeboat was, by now, well out of Ramsey Bay, and the confused seas were making conditions very difficult. After two attempts a towline was secured between lifeboat and yacht, and for a third time that night the lifeboat set course for Ramsey.

At dawn the weather improved and the wind dropped, enabling the lifeboat to make the final part of her third tow at full speed. Although this was the last yacht assisted by *James Ball Ritchie*, the 54ft Arun *The Gough-Ritchie*, from Port St Mary, was also launched to assist a yacht. The Port St Mary lifeboat could be seen from Ramsey as *James Ball Ritchie* returned to the beach to be recovered and re-housed.

Between the time she launched, late on 25 May, and the early morning of 26 May, *James Ball Ritchie* had helped fourteen yachtsmen and brought three yachts to safety. For this series of rescues, the Thanks on Vellum was accorded to Coxswain Kinnon; Vellum service certificates were presented to the crew, Second Coxswain Douglas Martin, Acting Mechanic Ronald Crowe, Emergency Mechanic Gerald Evison, and crew members Kevin Crowe, Alan Christian, Kim Holland and Anthony Gaines.

Disposal

James Ball Ritchie was kept at McAllisters Bt Yd, Dumbarton, as Emergency Relief until 12 February 1992 when she was declared non-operational. She was stored at Dumbarton until September 1992 and then totally destroyed (by burning) in accordance with the specific instructions of the RNLI.

Birds Eye

Official Number	984
Operational Number	37-25
Year built	1970
Builder	William Osborne, Littlehampton
Yard No.	WO 996
Cost	£38,500
Donor	Provided by Birds Eye Foods Ltd, Walton-on-Thames, Surrey, following their 'Help Launch a Lifeboat' campaign in the summer of 1969.
Named	9 September 1970 at New Quay by Alastair Graham, President of the New Quay RNLI Station Branch.

Stations

New Quay	July 1970 – Jan. 1990	90/42

Movements

16.7.1970 – 27.2.1979	New Quay (sl)
27.2.1979 – 21.6.1979	Holyhead Bt Yd, Anglesey (S, rlvd by ON.974 at New Quay)
21.6.1979 – 23.6.1979	Passage to New Quay
23.6.1979 – 27.4.1984	New Quay (sl)
27.4.1984 – 16.11.1984	Dickie's Bt Yd, Bangor (S, rlvd by ON.994 at New Quay)
16.11.1984 – 23.2.1990	New Quay (sl)
23.2.1990 – 24.2.1990	Passage to Dickie's Bt Yd, Bangor (via Port Dinorwic)
24.2.1990 – 6.3.1990	Dickie's Bt Yd, Bangor (S, hull found beyond economic repair)
6.3.1990 – 31.5.1991	Anglesey Bt Yd, Beaumaris (std)

Birds Eye on trials before going to New Quay. (RNLI)

Left and below:
Birds Eye at New
Quay during her
naming ceremony on
9 September 1970.
(Jeff Morris)

Notable Rescue

In the morning of 19 September 1973, *Birds Eye* was launched to the gaff-cutter *Susie Wong*, of Aberystwyth, which was seen to be in difficulties 1½ miles off the harbour. The wind was strong to near gale force and the lifeboat had to contend with rough seas as she made her way to the casualty.

The lifeboat reached the yacht half an hour after launching, but at first the three men on board the yacht refused help, saying they were on their way to Ireland. As the weather worsened the yacht was unable to make any headway, began drifting towards rocks and shipping water. After the engine broke down, her occupants agreed to be towed to harbour.

The lifeboatmen rigged a tow-rope and towed her back to New Quay. It later became clear that she had in fact been stolen from Aberystwyth harbour. Although relatively routine, this was typical of the many services carried out by *Birds Eye* during her service life at New Quay.

Disposal

Following a survey at Dickie's Bt Yd, Bangor, in 1990, the hull was found to be in such poor condition that *Birds Eye* was beyond economic repair. The boat was stored at Beaumaris until 31 May 1991, and then taken to the Sea Watch Centre, Moelfre, Anglesey, for permanent display inside.

Lady Murphy

Official Number	997
Operational Number	37–26
Year built	1971
Builder	William Osborne, Littlehampton
Yard No.	WO 18
Cost	£38,500
Donor	Legacy of the late Lady Frances Murphy, Dun Laoghaire, Co. Dublin.
Named	10 June 1972 by Mrs Brian Lenihan, wife of the Minister for Transport and Power, at Kilmore.

Lady Murphy on trials prior to going to Kilmore Quay for station duty.

Recovery of *Lady Murphy* at Kilmore Quay after the tragic capsize on Christmas Eve 1977.

Recovery of *Lady Murphy* on the beach at Kilmore Quay.

Stations

Kilmore Quay   Feb. 1972 – Sept. 1988   49/5

Movements

4.2.1972 – 24.12.1977	Kilmore Quay (sl)
24.12.1977 – 22.6.1978	Crosshaven Bt Yd, Crosshaven (S, fitted with radar)
22.6.1978 – 26.6.1978	Passage to Kilmore Quay
26.6.1978 – 1.5.1983	Kilmore Quay (sl)
1.5.1983 – 18.6.1983	Tyrrells Bt Yd, Arklow (S)
18.6.1983 – 10.12.1985	Kilmore Quay (sl)
10. 12.1985 – 11.12.1985	Passage to Dickie's Bt Yd, Bangor
11.12.1985 – 28.6.1986	Dickie's Bt Yd, Bangor (S)
28.6.1986 – 29.6.1986	Passage to Kilmore Quay
29.6.1986 – 26.9.1988	Kilmore Quay (sl)
26.9.1988 – 8.1995	Arklow (std)

Notable Rescue

While searching for reported distress flares on 24 December 1977, *Lady Murphy* capsized twice with the loss of crew member Finton Sinnott. Acting Second Coxswain Joseph Maddock and Acting Assistant Mechanic Dermot Cullerton were also injured during the capsize. The coxswain and mechanic, helped by other crew members, rescued one crew member who was washed out of the lifeboat during the first capsize and three of the four crew members washed out during the second capsize.

Following the events of Christmas Eve 1977, the Silver medal was awarded to Coxswain Thomas Walsh, the Bronze medal was awarded to Acting Mechanic John James Devereaux and the Thanks on Vellum was accorded to the remainder of the crew, Acting Second Coxswain Joseph Maddock, Acting Assistant Mechanic Dermot Culleton, David Culleton and Eugene Kehoe. A special certificate inscribed on vellum was awarded posthumously to Finton Sinnott.

Disposal

Lady Murphy was taken to Arklow on 26 September 1988 and, after inspection, was deemed unsuitable for sale. At one time she was to go on display at the Arklow Enterprise Centre, but was subsequently broken up at Arklow Marine & Leisure Ltd, Arklow, during the summer of 1995.

Rothers

Osman Gabriel

Official Number	998
Operational Number	37–27
Year built	1972
Builder	William Osborne, Littlehampton
Yard No.	WO 19
Cost	£60,000
Donor	Gift of Major Osman B. Gabriel, Hove.
Named	4 August 1973 at Port Erin by Mrs D. Maddrell, Chair of the Port Erin Ladies Lifeboat Guild.

Stations
Port Erin	July 1973 – June 1992	70/55
Relief	1992 – 1993	0/0

Movements
1.7.1973 – 24.9.1978	Port Erin (sl)
24.9.1978 – 24.2.1979	Holyhead Bt Yd (S, rlvd by ON.974)
24.2.1979 – 8.1.1984	Port Erin (sl)
8.1.1984 – 9.1.1984	Passage to McGruers Bt Yd, Helensburgh
9.1.1984 – 7.7.1984	McGruers Bt Yd, Helensburgh (S, rlvd by ON.984)
7.7.1984 – 8.7.1984	Passage to Port Erin

Osman Gabriel displayed on the RNLI stand at the Earls Court Boat Show, London, 1973. (Jeff Morris)

Launch of *Osman Gabriel* down the slipway on exercise at Port Erin in July 1989. (Tony Denton)

The first Rother, *Osman Gabriel*, at sea off Port Erin. (From a photograph supplied by David Gooch)

8.7.1984 – 14.8.1988	Port Erin (sl)
14.8.1988 – 16.8.1988	Passage to McAlisters Bt Yd, Dumbarton
16.8.1988 – 11.2.1989	McAlisters Bt Yd, Dumbarton (S, rlvd by ON.1022: 2/0)
11.2.1989 – 21.2.1989	Passage to Port Erin (weatherbound at Troon on 20.2.1989 on passage)
21.2.1989 – 2.3.1992	Port Erin (sl)
2.3.1992 – 4.3.1992	Passage to Dumbarton
4.3.1992 – 5.6.1992	McAlisters Bt Yd, Dumbarton (rlvd by ON.1047)
5.6.1992 – 6.6.1992	Passage to Port Erin
6.6.1992 – 22.6.1992	Port Erin (sl)
22.6.1992 – 23.6.1992	Dickies Bt Yd, Bangor (withdrawn, station temporarily closed from 22.6.1992 for adaptation of boathouse in readiness for a new Atlantic 21)
23.6.1992-24.6.1992	Passage to Poole (by road)
24.6.1992-1.3.1993	RNLI Depot, Poole (ER; for disposal)

Recovery of *Osman Gabriel* after exercise, July 1989. (Tony Denton)

Notable Rescues

On 28 March 1978, *Osman Gabriel* was launched from the slipway at Port Erin under the command of Coxswain Peter Woodworth to an inflatable dinghy with four people on board. Half an hour after launching, the casualty was sighted at the base of a 700ft cliff near Fleshwick Bay. The lifeboat was taken in to the cliffs where a small boat was pulled out of the water, with three skin divers close by and a fourth climbing the cliff to get help. The lifeboat stood by the three men and started to initiate a rescue using the breeches buoy.

At first the three divers tried to transfer their boat and diving gear onto the lifeboat, but were unable to do so because it was too heavy. As they struggled with the boat, the weather deteriorated and the wind increased to force six. The light was fading and Coxswain Woodworth was becoming concerned about the safety of the stranded men.

More than two hours after arriving on the scene, the divers were instructed to abandon attempts to save their gear and prepare to be rescued themselves. All three of them were rescued using the breeches buoy within twenty minutes, after which the lifeboat headed back to Port Erin. During the return passage the lifeboat headed into very rough breaking seas, with the wind by now blowing a near gale, force seven.

For this rescue the Thanks on Vellum was accorded to Coxswain Woodworth; Vellum service certificates were presented to the rest of the crew. Throughout the rescue, the coxswain had to manoeuvre the lifeboat skilfully to ensure she did not strike submerged rocks, at times only 6ft away.

Disposal

Osman Gabriel was placed on a sale list in January 1993 and sold out of service on 1 March 1993 to the Estonian Lifeboat Service. She left the RNLI Depot, Poole, by road on 11 March 1993 and arrived at Felixstowe the following day for shipping out to the former Soviet state of Estonia to continue her lifesaving duties there. Although the Estonian Lifeboat Service had been anxious to add to its fleet, funding was difficult. An approach was therefore made to the British Embassy in Tallin for assistance, as a result of which the Foreign Office agreed to the Ambassador's recommendation that funds be made available to buy the lifeboat from the RNLI.

Diana White

Official Number	999
Operational Number	37-28
Year built	1973
Builder	William Osborne, Littlehampton
Yard No.	WO 20
Cost	£89,000
Donor	The Cornish Lifeboat Appeal and an anonymous gift.
Named	19 July 1974 at Sennen Cove by HRH Duke of Kent.

Stations

Sennen Cove	Nov. 1973 – 1991	80/64

Movements

1.11.1973 – 28.11.1977	Sennen Cove (sl)
28.11.1977 – 15.4.1978	Mashford's Bt Yd, Plymouth (R, Ovh, rlvd by ON.994)
15.4.1978 – 22.10.1981	Sennen Cove (sl)
22.10.1981 – 15.5.1982	Falmouth Boat Co. (S, rlvd by ON.994)
15.5.1982 – 21.12.1986	Sennen Cove (sl)
21.12.1986 – 30.3.1988	Mashford's Bt Yd, Plymouth (S, rlvd by ON.1064)
30.4.1988 – 10.4.1991	Sennen Cove (sl)
10.4.1991 – 18.9.1991	Falmouth Boat Co. (S, rlvd by ON.1022)
18.9.1991 – 19.9.1991	Passage to RNLI Depot, Poole (withdrawn from Sennen Cove)
19.9.1991 – 15.6.1992	RNLI Depot, Poole (std; placed on sale list 18.3.1992)
15.6.1992	Declared non-operational

Diana White at William Osborne's boatyardd, Littlehampton. (Jeff Morris)

Diana White moored at Cremyll, near Plymouth, on 28 March 1988 following a survey at Mashford's Bt Yd. (Tony Denton)

Notable Rescues

While serving at Sennen Cove, *Diana White* was involved in two notable rescues which earned her coxswains the Silver medal. The first took place on 16 November 1977 and involved not only Sennen Cove's lifeboat, but also the 37ft Oakley *Frank Penfold Marshall* from St Ives. *Diana White* was launched to the cargo vessel *Union Crystal*, of Singapore, which was in trouble in a strong gale, rain squalls and high seas.

The launch from the slipway at Sennen Cove was extremely difficult, as the conditions exceeded those which had always in the past been recognised as the limit for launching. Nevertheless, Coxswain/Mechanic Eric Pengilly decided that they must try. At 7.43 p.m. the lifeboat was launched and, as soon as she entered the water, was hit by short, steep waves which began to turn her to starboard. Many onlookers thought she had been driven ashore.

Coxswain/Mechanic Pengilly struggled to control the boat, and she was seen to be 'stood on end' by several eyewitnesses. However, with help from Acting Second Coxswain Maurice Hutchens and crew member Phillip Shannon, the coxswain just maintained control of the boat.

Diana White then ploughed through the surf on the bar and set out into the force ten gale. Together with *Frank Penfold Marshall* from St Ives, she searched under the direction of the tanker *Texaco Great Britain*, which was coordinating the operation. By 9.30 p.m., when HMS *Penelope* arrived on scene to act as on-scene commander, six ships, two lifeboats and two helicopters were involved. At 10.34 p.m. a life raft, containing one survivor, and wreckage was spotted.

At 11.17 p.m. the Sennen Cove lifeboat was recalled to station as the area was well saturated with search craft. She had been at sea for nearly six hours searching for survivors in appalling conditions. Indeed, conditions were too bad for her to be recovered at Sennen, so she made for Newlyn, where she arrived at 1.20 a.m. on 17 November.

For this service, the Silver medal was awarded to Coxswain/Mechanic Pengilly. The Thanks on Vellum was accorded to Emergency Mechanic Hedley Hutchings, Acting Second Coxswain Hutchens, and crew members Phillip Shannon, John Chope, John Pender, and Cedric Johnson. The lifeboat was slightly damaged during the service and so was taken off service and relieved by *Vincent Nesfield* (ON.994). Sadly, Pengilly died in January 1978, a few weeks after the service. The Thanks on Vellum was accorded to Coxswain Thomas Cocking, Snr, of the St Ives lifeboat, and Vellum service certificates were presented to the rest of the St Ives crew.

The second Silver medal service in which *Diana White* was involved took place on 19 September 1981. She was launched to the Icelandic coaster *Tungufoss* in difficulties four miles south of Longships lighthouse, with eight men on board. The coaster was listing 40 degrees to port after her cargo of maize had shifted in a south-westerly gale and a very rough sea.

Once on the scene, the lifeboat found that three men had been lifted off by a helicopter. Another three had got into life rafts at the stern of the casualty, and as the life rafts floated towards the lifeboat, they were recovered. Two more men were pulled from the water after they had missed life rafts, and another two were taken off the coaster itself. Coxswain Maurice Hutchens took the lifeboat in alongside *Tungufoss* approximately twenty times in order to effect the rescue from the coaster, which heeled over further and further throughout. The last two crewmembers were taken off when the vessel had a list of 60 degrees. Once all the crew had been saved, the lifeboat set a course for her station. The casualty eventually foundered and sank south of Gwennap Head.

For this outstanding rescue, the Silver medal was awarded to Coxswain/Mechanic Hutchens in recognition of his courage, leadership and seamanship; medal service certificates were presented to the remainder of the crew. On 17 February 1982, the President of Iceland, Mrs Vigdis Finnbogadottir, presented the Republic of Iceland's silver medal for valour to Coxswain/Mechanic Hutchens at a special ceremony.

Disposal

Diana White was sold in 1992 to Sumner Lifeboat Institution, New Zealand; she was taken by road to Southampton on 15 June 1992 for shipment onboard a P&O container vessel on 19 June. After being offloaded at Lyttelton she was immediately launched into New Zealand waters amid great excitement on 5 August 1992. She replaced a former RNLI Liverpool class lifeboat, *Rescue III* (ON.914), which was sold by Sumner. *Diana White* was then accompanied by the other two rescue boats at Sumner, jetboat *Caroline Nicholson* and IRB *Lady Frances*, on trials in the bay. On Sunday 8 November 1992, she was officially named *Joseph Day* by Dame Catherine Tizard, Governor General of Christchurch, and was used as a lifeboat in New Zealand. In 1999, she was replaced by another ex-RNLI lifeboat, ON.1032, and was sold by Sumner for approximately NZ$55,000 to a private owner who reverted her name to *Diana White* and used her as a pleasure boat based at Tauranaga, Bay of Plenty.

Mary Gabriel

Official Number	1000
Operational Number	37-29
Year built	1974
Builder	William Osborne, Littlehampton
Yard No.	WO 21
Cost	£90,000
Donor	Gift of Major Osman B. Gabriel, Hove.
Named	2 May 1974 at Shoreham Harbour by Lady Egremont, President of the Ladies Lifeboat Guild, in the presence of Major and Mrs Gabriel; Mrs Gabriel was unwell and so could not travel to Hoylake for a ceremony dedicated there on 2 June 1974.

Stations

Hoylake	May 1974 – Oct. 1990	99*/44
Rhyl	Dec. 1990 – Apr. 1992	7/0

*Including one which took place on 1 May 1974 to a yacht and two dinghies while on trials out of Shoreham, before being delivered to Hoylake, but with Hoylake crew aboard.

Movements

17.5.1974 – 20.7.1979	Hoylake (sl)
20.7.1979 – 30.11.1979	Holyhead Bt Yd (S)
30.11.1979 – 22.5.1982	Hoylake (sl)
22.5.1982 – 14.7.1982	Holyhead Bt Yd (S)
14.7.1982 – 18.2.1988	Hoylake (sl)

Mary Gabriel on trials prior to going on station at Hoylake.

Mary Gabriel
launching on
exercise at
Hoylake. (Tony
Denton)

Mary Gabriel
on the
launchway
onto the
beach at
Hoylake in
October
1990.
(Nicholas
Leach)

18.2.1988 – 6.9.1988	Anglesey Bt Yd, Beaumaris (S, rlvd by ON.942)
6.9.1988 – 13.10.1990	Hoylake (sl)
13.10.1990 – 23.12.1990	Dickie's Bt Yd, Bangor (S, replaced at Hoylake by ON.1163)
23.12.1990 – 6.4.1992	Rhyl (replacing ON.993; taken off service on 2.4.1992 due to hull damage suffered whilst on service; rlvd by ON.1022 on 3.4.1992 and sent by road transport for R to be carried out at RNLI Depot, Poole)
6.4.1992 – 7.4.1992	Passage by road transport to Poole
7.4.1992 – 31.10.1992	RNLI Depot, Poole (std, then placed on sale list; hull damage too severe to warrant repair)
31.10.1992	Declared non-operational

Disposal

Mary Gabriel was sold on 31 October 1992 and left the RNLI Depot, Poole, on 16 November 1992. She had been bought by owners in Northamptonshire and was kept on the River Nene at Peterborough, unaltered. During 1994 she spent the summer at Wells having been at Orton Mere, Nene Park, Peterborough, on the River Nene. In 1997 she went up to Burgh Castle Marina where she stayed for a fortnight, still painted in RNLI livery. She was taken to Wells regularly, and was present in August 1998 for a rally of ex lifeboats. In 2001, she was given to the National Lifeboat Collection at Chatham Historic Dockyard as a floating exhibit. On 3 June 2001 she arrived at Chatham having been brought from Wells by a group of Chatham volunteers. She is now moored in the River Medway alongside Thunderbolt Pier, next to the Dockyard.

Harold Salvesen

Official Number	1022
Operational Number	37–30
Year built	1974
Builder	Groves & Guttridge, Cowes
Yard No.	G&G 656
Cost	£90,000
Donor	Gift of the Salvesen Trust.
Named	6 September 1975 at Amble by Mrs Salvesen.

Harold Salvesen at moorings alongside Radcliffe Quay, Amble, where she served for twelve years. (Jeff Morris)

Harold Salvesen at Bridlington in July 1986. She was too large to fit inside the lifeboat house and so was kept in the open on the promenade. (Paul Russell)

Stations

Amble	Jun. 1974 – Jun. 1986	61/6
Relief	Jun. 1986 – Jun. 1992	33/4
Rhyl	Apr. 1992 – Jun. 1992	1/0

Movements

8.6.1974 – 20.5.1975	Amble (sl)
20.5.1975 – 12.12.1975	Amble Bt Co. Ltd (rlvd by ON.848)
12.12.1975 – 18.5.1978	Amble (sl)
18.5.1978 – 12.7.1978	Amble Bt Co. Ltd (rlvd by ON.858)
12.7.1978 – 3.4.1981	Amble (sl)
3.4.1981 – 31.8.1981	Amble Bt Co. Ltd (rlvd by ON.868)
31.8.1981 – 9.4.1983	Amble (sl)
9.4.1983 – 5.7.1983	Amble Bt Co. Ltd (rlvd by ON.934)
5.7.1983 – 6.3.1985	Amble (sl)
6.3.1985 – 5.6.1985	Amble Bt Co. Ltd (rlvd by ON.967)
5.6.1985 – 8.6.1986	Amble (sl)
8.6.1986 – 9.6.1986	Amble (ER; withdrawn when new lifeboat ON.1004 at station)
9.6.1986–11.7.1986	Leggett's Yard, Grimsby (S; carriage hooks fitted for Relief Fleet; Bridlington relieving ON.867 enabling ON.972 Flamborough to go for S; with adequate cover in the area, no replacement at Flamborough)

11.7.1986 – 5.12.1986	Bridlington (rlvg ON.867, ON.980 station boat with-drawn for complete hull S after damage; 6/0)
5.12.1986 – 4.9.1987	Filey (rlvg ON.966, 10/1 life)
4.9.1987 – 5.9.1987	Passage to Leggett's Yard, Grimsby
5.9.1987 – 21.3.1988	Leggett's Yard, Grimsby (S)
21.3.1988 – 11.7.1988	Arbroath (rlvg ON.1054: 0/0)
11.7.1988 – 13.7.1988	Montrose (hauled out, off-loaded for transporting to Berthon Boat Co.)
13.7.1988 – 14.7.1988	Passage by road to Lymington
14.7.1988 – 4.8.1988	Berthon Boat Co., Lymington (S)
4.8.1988 – 8.8.1988	RNLI Depot, Poole (ER)
8.8.1988 – 11.8.1988	Passage by road to Workington, off-loaded, launched to sail to Port Erin
11.8.1988 – 12.8.1988	Arrived at Workington and sailed to Port Erin for relief
12.8.1988 – 13.2.1989	Port Erin (rlvg ON.998: 2/0)
13.2.1989 – 14.2.1989	Holyhead Bt Yd (I)
14.2.1989 – 24.2.1989	Barmouth (rlvg ON.1063: 0/0)
24.2.1989 – 9.4.1989	Anglesey Bt Yd, Beaumaris (R to hull leaks)
9.4.1989 – 2.9.1989	Barmouth (rlvg ON.1063, 8/0)
2.9.1989 – 7.10.1990	Anglesey Bt Yd, Beaumaris (ER, Ovh)
7.10.1990 – 23.1.1991	Barmouth (rlvg ON.1063: 1/3)
23.1.1991 – 6.4.1991	Anglesey Bt Yd, Beaumaris (ER, S)
6.4.1991 – 9.4.1991	Passage to Sennen Cove (via Beaumaris 6.4.91, Holyhead 7.4.91, Fishguard 8.4.91, Padstow and Sennen 9.4.91)

Harold Salvesen launching at Rhyl in June 1992 to meet the station's new 12m Mersey *Lil Cunningham*. (Nicholas Leach)

Harold Salvesen leaving Rhyl harbour in June 1992. (Nicholas Leach)

9.4.1991 – 9.10.1991	Sennen Cove (rlvg ON.999; on moorings during shore-works: 6/0)
9.10.1991 – 12.10.1991	Passage to ABC (Sennen Cove station temporarily closed while shorework taking place and awaiting arrival of new sl ON.1176)
12.10.1991 – 16.1.1992	Anglesey Bt Yd, Beaumaris (ER)
16.1.1992 – 18.3.1992	Barmouth (rlvg ON.1063)
18.3.1992 – 19.3.1992	Passage overnight to Beaumaris
19.3.1992 – 3.4.1992	Anglesey Bt Yd, Beaumaris (ER)
3.4.1992 – 23.6.1992	Rhyl (TSD: 1/0)
23.6.1992 – 29.6.1992	Rhyl (awaiting passage)
29.6.1992 – 30.6.1992	Passage to RNLI Depot, Poole (overnight by road)
30.6.1992 – 16.10.1992	RNLI Depot, Poole (std, placed on sale list 11.7.1992)

Disposal

Sold on 16 October 1992 and transported from Poole Depot on 10 November 1992. Re-sold on 10 February 1994, moved to the River Tawe Marina, Swansea, named *TSMV Salvesen*, but unaltered externally. She was kept at Swansea until 1998, when she was moved to the Floating Dock, Bristol, then in 2000 to Instow on the River Torridge. She later moved to Pembroke Dock for Winter 2001-2002 where she was refurbished, and then taken to Mylor, Cornwall, in 2002.

J. Reginald Corah

Official Number	1023
Operational Number	37–31
Year built	1975
Builder	Groves & Guttridge, Cowes
Yard No.	G&G 657
Cost	£95,000
Donor	Gift of the J. Reginald Corah Foundation Fund, Corah Ltd of Leicester.
Named	6 May 1976 at Swanage.

Stations

Swanage	Oct. 1975 – Nov. 1991	410/240

Movements

1.1.1975 – 30.10.1979	Swanage (sl)
30.10.1979 – 16.2.1980	Wm Osborne, Littlehampton (S)
16.2.1980 – 20.9.1984	Swanage (sl)
20.9.1984 – 8.3.1985	Cantell's Bt Yd, Newhaven (S, rlvd by ON.942)
8.3.1985 – 20.11.1988	Swanage (sl)
20.11.1988 – 21.11.1988	Passage (weatherbound at Poole, rlvd by ON.1047)
21.11.1988 – 22.11.1988	Passage to Newhaven
22.11.1988 – 6.6.1990	Cantell's Bt Yd, Newhaven (S)
6.6.1990 – 7.6.1990	Passage to Swanage
7.6.1990 – 23.5.1991	Swanage (sl)
23.5.1991 – 24.5.1991	RNLI Depot, Poole, awaiting repairs
24.5.1991 – 6.8.1991	Branksea Marine, Wareham (R, rlvd by ON.1064)

Launch of *J. Reginald Corah* on 1 July 1986 for BBC television's *Songs of Praise*. (Jeff Morris)

J. Reginald Corah at Swanage during the station's annual Lifeboat Day in July 1984. (Nicholas Leach)

6.8.1991 – 27.11.1991	Swanage (sl; withdrawn for repairs, did not return to Swanage)
27.11.1991 – 9.12.1991	RNLI Depot, Poole (hull repairs to leaks; Swanage temporarily without a lifeboat)
9.12.1991 – 6.5.1992	Branksea Marine, Wareham (R)
6.5.1992 – 21.7.1995	RNLI Depot, Poole (std, for sale)

Notable Rescues

During her time stationed at Swanage, *J. Reginald Corah* performed several notable rescues for which her crew received formal recognition from the RNLI. On three occasions the Thanks Inscribed on Vellum was accorded to her crews. The first of these Vellum services took place on 24 September 1976 when she assisted a yacht in difficulties and escorted the motor cruiser *Zare*. The Thanks on Vellum was accorded to Coxswain Ronald Hardy and Emergency Mechanic Philip Dorey for their part in the rescue. The second service took place on 19 September 1981 to the motor fishing vessel *Outlaw* from which one person was rescued. The Thanks on Vellum was accorded to Coxswain Philip Dorey. On 22 January 1988, *J. Reginald Corah* performed another service, to the cargo vessel *Renee*, of Malta, which was in difficulties in heavy seas ten miles off Anvil Point. The vessel was escorted into Swanage Bay, for which the Thanks on Vellum was accorded to Coxswain/Mechanic Vic Marsh and Emergency Mechanic Martin Steedman.

However, the most exceptional service undertaken by *J. Reginald Corah* at Swanage took place on 14 October 1976, only a few months after she had been formally named and dedicated. She was launched, with Coxswain Ron Hardy in command, in exceptionally bad weather to the Russian trawler *Topaz*, which was heading for Swanage Bay with the French yacht *Campscharles* in tow, having taken the yacht's crew of two on board. The lifeboat had been requested to take over the tow although no lives were in immediate danger.

J. Reginald Corah on the slipway at Swanage in July 1987. (Tony Denton)

The lifeboat approached *Topaz* at 1.30 p.m. and Coxswain Hardy took her alongside. In the extremely heavy seas, the lifeboat sustained some damage, but bow and stern lines were secured and the yacht's two crewmembers were able to jump onto the lifeboat. The towline from the trawler to the yacht was passed to the lifeboatmen by the Russian seamen. The lifeboat was suffering further damage to her port side, so the lines were let go and the lifeboat backed away. As the lifeboat went astern, however, the towline fouled her rudder and starboard propeller. The yacht was immediately cut adrift and the rope was cleared from the lifeboat's rudder. Attempts to clear the starboard propeller failed, despite repeated efforts using the equipment onboard the lifeboat designed specifically for the purpose, and the lifeboat had to continue on one engine.

She then set off to catch up with the yacht, which had drifted some distance away. Lifeboatman Chris Haw was put on board the yacht when it was reached and, once a towline was secured, the yacht was taken into Poole harbour and moored. The lifeboat also stayed there until the following afternoon, as it was impossible to re-house at Swanage.

For this outstanding service, Bronze medals were awarded to both Coxswain Ronald Hardy, his second such award, and Second Coxswain/Mechanic Vic Marsh.

Disposal

J. Reginald Corah was sold on 21 July 1995 and left the RNLI Depot, Poole, by sea, sailing on the 10.30 a.m. bridge for Chichester harbour manned by a new owner and his own crew. She was renamed *Louise*, but has remained largely unaltered and is kept at Chichester Marina.

The Hampshire Rose

Official Number	999
Operational Number	37–32
Year built	1974
Builder	William Osborne, Littlehampton
Yard No.	WO 22/1024
Cost	£95,000
Donor	The Hampshire Rose Appeal, launched in 1973 by Sir Alec Rose, together with RNLI funds. Handing-over ceremony took place in the presence of HM the Queen Mother on 1 June 1975.
Named	6 September 1975 at Walmer by Lady Rose, wife of Sir Alec Rose.

Stations

Walmer	Feb. 1975 – May 1990	132/57
Relief	1990 – 1992	14/2

Movements

1.1.1973 – 1.9.1974	Wm Osborne, Littlehampton (building, adapted for beach launching at Walmer)
1.9.1974 – 27.1.1975	Wm Osborne, Littlehampton (T)
27.1.1975 – 1.2.1975	Passage to Walmer
1.2.1975 – 3.2.1975	Walmer
3.2.1975 – 4.5.1975	Walmer (sl)

The Hampshire Rose on the launching cradle at the head of Walmer beach. The lifeboat house, used at this time for the inshore lifeboat, can be seen in the background. (From an old postcard in the author's collection)

The Hampshire Rose at Walmer. (From a postcard supplied by Mark Roberts)

4.5.1975 – 30.5.1975	Denton Shiprepairers, Otterham Quay (rlvd by ON.948, preparation for naming ceremony)
30.5.1975 – 2.6.1975	Portsmouth (for handing-over ceremony, rlvd by ON.948)
2.6.1975 – 28.6.1975	Passage on coastal trials
28.6.1975 – 14.6.1976	Walmer (sl)
14.6.1976 – 20.7.1976	Denton Shiprepairers Ltd, Otterham Quay (rlvd by ON.948)
20.7.1976 – 4.7.1977	Walmer (sl)
23.9.1976	Attended naming of new Ramsgate lifeboat *Ralph and Joy Swann*
4.7.1977 – 8.8.1977	Brown's Bt Yd, Rowhedge (rlvd by ON.859)
8.8.1977 – 28.6.1978	Walmer (sl)
28.6.1978 – 18.8.1978	Brown's Bt Yd, Rowhedge (rlvd by ON.859)
18.8.1978 – 8.10.1979	Walmer (sl)
8.10.1979 – 8.2.1980	Dan, Webb & Feesey (rlvd by ON.937)
8.2.1980 – 22.10.1981	Walmer (sl)
22.10.1981 – 12.2.1982	Brown's Bt Yd, Rowhedge (rlvd by ON.937)
12.2.1982 – 14.2.1983	Walmer (sl)
14.2.1983 – 26.6.1983	Denton Shiprepairers, Otterham Quay (rlvd by ON.948)
26.6.1983 – 30.10.1983	Walmer (sl)
30.10.1983 – 1.11.1983	Whisstocks Yard, Woodbridge (rlvd by ON.948: 0/0)
1.11.1983 – 24.9.1984	Walmer (sl)
24.9.1984 – 9.12.1984	Whisstocks Yard, Woodbridge (rlvd by ON.948)
9.12.1984 – 8.10.1985	Walmer (sl)

8.10.1985 – 8.5.1986	Fletchers Bt Yd, Lowestoft (rlvd by ON.948)
8.5.1986 – 8.7.1987	Walmer (sl)
8.7.1987 – 8.5.1988	Fletchers Bt Yd, Lowestoft (rlvd by ON.948)
8.5.1988 – 7.9.1989	Walmer (sl)
7.9.1989 – 9.9.1989	Passage to Fletchers
9.9.1989 – 18.2.1990	Fletchers Bt Yd, Lowestoft (rlvd by ON.1048)
18.2.1990 – 6.5.1990	Walmer (sl, withdrawn 6.5.1990, station to operate Atlantic 21)
6.5.1990 – 9.5.1990	Passage to Poole Depot
9.5.1990 – 10.5.1990	RNLI Poole Depot
10.5.1990 – 14.12.1990	Branksea Marine, Wareham (S, moved to Salterns Marine; road to Buckie)
14.12.1990 – 9.3.1991	Jones' Yard, Buckie (awaiting passage)

The Hampshire Rose beaching at Walmer with a 42ft Watson lifeboat visible in the background. (From a postcard supplied by Mark Roberts)

The Hampshire Rose on relief duty at Anstruther in August 1991. (Tony Denton)

9.3.1991 – 10.3.1991	Passage to Anstruther (via Aberdeen)
10.3.1991 – 22.11.1991	Anstruther (relieving ON.983: 8/0; until 17.10.1991 when replaced by ON.1174; became ER)
22.11.1991 – 24.11.1991	Passage to Herd & Mackenzie, Buckie (std)
24.11.1991 – 29.11.1991	Herd & Mackenzie, Buckie (std)
29.11.1991 – 1.12.1991	Passage by road transport to Poole
1.12.1991 – 2.12.1991	RNLI Depot, Poole
2.12.1991 – 13.6.1992	Swanage (relieving ON.1023, 6/2)
13.6.1992 – 31.10.1992	RNLI Depot, Poole (ER, std from 19.6.1992; on sale list 11.7.1992)

Notable Rescues

On 10 December 1977, *The Hampshire Rose* was launched under Coxswain Bruce Brown from the beach at Walmer after reports of ship's lights in the vicinity of the East Goodwin Buoy. The wind was strong breeze to near gale, force six to seven, with steep high seas and heavy rain. Once in the water, at 11.00 p.m., the lifeboat was forced to reduce speed in the confused and heavy seas, which were breaking over the boat and making navigation and handling extremely difficult.

Despite the radar being unusable, as it had developed a fault, the lifeboat found a large cargo vessel fast on the Goodwin Sands. The casualty, the cargo vessel *Elmela* of Greece, had a heavy list to starboard and was anchored with a crew of twenty-five on board. Coxswain Brown managed to get Second Coxswain Cyril Williams on board, by skilfully taking the lifeboat alongside the vessel despite the heavy seas.

The master of the cargo vessel declined offers to order tugs or evacuate the crew and so the lifeboat stood by as the tide ebbed. At 4.05 a.m. on 11 December, the Ramsgate lifeboat, the 44ft Waveney *Ralph and Joy Swann* (ON.1042), was launched to assist *Hampshire Rose*. She arrived at 4.59 a.m. and, after agreeing that *Elmela* was firmly settled until the next rising tide, the Walmer lifeboat left for her station.

The Hampshire Rose beached at Walmer at 7.15 a.m., refuelled and re-launched at 8.45 a.m. The wind and sea conditions were by now moderating and, at 9.15 a.m., the *Elmela* began to move with the rising tide. A line was run from the ship's bow to the Ramsgate lifeboat, and gradually the casualty was pulled clear of the shoal area. Escorted by the Ramsgate lifeboat, *Elmela* made for Margate Roads.

The Walmer lifeboat had taken Second Coxswain Williams aboard again by 10.00 a.m., and she then returned to station before midday. For this service, framed letters of thanks signed by Major-General Ralph Farrant, Chairman of the Institution, were sent to Coxswain Brown and Second Coxswain/Assistant Mechanic Williams. Letters of thanks signed by the RNLI Director, Captain Nigel Dixon, were sent to Second Coxswain/Assistant Mechanic Derek Pegden and crew member Anthony Read of the Ramsgate lifeboat.

Disposal

The Hampshire Rose was subsequently sold out of service on 31 October 1992 to an owner on the South Coast. She was resold and moved to Monkston Marina near Swansea, where she was kept unaltered in use as a pleasure boat. In 2000 she was moved to Plymouth under new ownership and kept at Mountbatten.

Silver Jubilee (Civil Service No.38)

Official Number	1046
Operational Number	37-33
Year built	1977
Builder	William Osborne, Littlehampton
Yard No.	WO 1117
Cost	£105,000
Donor	Civil Service and Post Office Lifeboat Fund.
Named	21 November 1979 at Margate by HRH Princess Margaret.

Stations

Margate	Nov. 1977 – Dec. 1991	165★/76
Relief	1991 – 1993	0/0

★Including one service while on trials out of Margate on 30.9.1978, when the fishing boat *Manta* of Littlehampton was escorted to harbour.

Movements

1.1.1977 – 18.9.1978	William Osborne, Littlehampton (uc)
18.9.1978 – 30.9.1978	William Osborne, Littlehampton (T)
30.9.1978 – 2.10.1978	Passage to Margate
2.10.1978 – 12.10.1978	Margate (CT)
12.10.1978 – 17.11.1978	Margate (restricted service)
17.11.1978 – 21.3.1981	Margate (sl, officially on service from 1700 on 21.3.81)
21.3.1981 – 24.4.1981	Brown's Bt Yd, Rowhedge (rlvd by ON.961)
24.4.1981 – 1.9.1985	Margate (sl)
1.9.1985 – 7.9.1985	Brown's Bt Yd, Rowhedge (I, no cover at station)
7.9.1985 – 21.10.1985	Margate (sl)
21.10.1985 – 25.10.1985	Local slipway (off service)
25.10.1985 – 7.8.1986	Crescent Shipyard, Otterham Quay (rlvd by ON.942;

Silver Jubilee (Civil Service No.38) on exercise off Margate. (From a postcard in the author's collection)

Silver Jubilee (Civil Service No.33) at sea off Margate. (From a postcard in the author's collection)

Silver Jubilee (Civil Service No.33) at Margate. (Ray Noble)

	withdrawn from 21.10.1985, no lifeboat at Margate until relief ON.942; ON.1046 withdrawn prematurely for full S to investigate a defect in a small portion of her hull)
7.8.1986 – 13.6.1990	Margate (sl; on 24.5.1990 escorted small boats at Dunkirk 50th anniversary from Dover with ON.1160, ON.1031 and ON.1154)
13.6.1990 – 14.6.1990	Passage to Crescent Shipyard
14.6.1990 – 23.10.1990	Crescent Shipyard, Otterham Quay (S, rlvd by ON.1047)
23.10.1990 – 19.12.1991	Margate (sl)
19.12.1991 – 20.12.1991	Margate (withdrawn, new lifeboat ON.1177 at Margate)
20.12.1991 – 23.12.1991	Passage to Otterham Quay
23.12.1991 – 16.1.1992	Crescent Shipyard, Otterham Quay (S, re-allocated to Relief)

16.1.1992 – 17.1.1992	Passage to Dungeness
17.1.1992 – 6.2.1992	Dungeness (rlvd ON.1048: 0/0)
6.2.1992 – 27.1.1993	Cantell's Bt Yd, Newhaven (ER)
27.1.1993 – 7.3.1994	RNLI Depot, Poole (by road transport, std 5.2.1993 and for sale)
7.3.1994 – 29.5.1994	RNLI Depot, Poole (non-operational, sold)

Disposal

Silver Jubilee (Civil Service No.38) was sold on 4 March 1994 to a buyer in Co. Dublin, Republic of Ireland; she left Poole on 29 May 1994 and was taken by sea under her new owner to East Ferry, Cork harbour. She was kept here for about a year, renamed *Catherie*, and used as a pleasure boat occasionally visiting Skerries harbour. About a year later she was moved to the Old Court Boat Yard, south of Skibbereen, Co. Cork, in south-west Ireland.

Horace Clarkson

Official Number	1047
Operational Number	37–34
Year built	1977
Builder	William Osborne, Littlehampton
Yard No.	WO 1118
Cost	£107,000
Donor	Clarkson Shipping & Insurance Group on the occasion of their 125th anniversary.
Named	18 June 1977 at Littlehampton by Mrs Renske Kemp after the founder of H. Clarkson (Holdings) Ltd, who funded the boat to commemorate the company's 125th anniversary. Re-dedicated 17 June 1978 at Moelfre by The Archbishop of Wales, The Most Reverend Gwilym Owen Williams.

Horace Clarkson inside the lifeboat house at Margate while on relief duty there in September 1990. (Paul Russell)

Horace Clarkson on relief at Dungeness. (Tony Denton)

Stations

| Moelfre | Oct. 1977 – Nov. 1986 | 55/21 |
| Relief | 1986 – 1993 | 49/37 |

Movements

14.10.1977 – 15.7.1982	Moelfre (sl)
15.7.1982 – 20.11.1982	Dickie's Bt Yd, Bangor (rlvd by ON.994)
20.11.1982 – 3.11.1986	Moelfre (sl)
3.11.1986 – 31.1.1987	Dickie's Bt Yd, Bangor (S)
31.1.1987 – 1.2.1987	Passage to Ilfracombe
1.2.1987 – 8.12.1987	Ilfracombe (rlvg ON.986, 8/13)
8.12.1987 – 11.12.1987	Passage to Littlehampton
11.12.1987 – 20.12.1987	Wm Osborne, Littlehampton (ER)
20.12.1987 – 18.5.1988	Dungeness (relieving ON.1048: 4/1)
18.5.1988 – 20.11.1988	Cantell's Bt Yd, Newhaven (ER, S, HC 19.11.1988)
20.11.1988 – 7.6.1990	Swanage (rlvg ON.1023: 28/22)
7.6.1990 – 11.6.1990	RNLI Depot, Poole
11.6.1990 – 13.6.1990	Passage to Margate
13.6.1990 – 23.10.1990	Margate (rlvg ON.1046: 4/0)
23.10.1990 – 22.4.1991	Denton Shiprepairers Ltd, Otterham Quay (S)
22.4.1991 – 24.4.1991	Passage to Dungeness (via Sheerness 22.4.91, Ramsgate 23.4.91, arriving at Dungeness 24.4.91)
24.4.1991 – 2.8.1991	Dungeness (rlvg ON.1048: 2/0)
2.8.1991 – 3.8.1991	Passage to Crescent Marine
3.8.1991 – 19.8.1991	Crescent Marine, Otterham Quay (S)
19.8.1991 – 22.8.1991	Passage to Buckie (by road)
22.8.1991 – 21.9.1991	Herd & Mackenzie, Buckie (I)
21.9.1991 – 22.9.1991	Passage to Arbroath
22.9.1991 – 14.12.1991	Arbroath (relieving ON.1054: 0/0)
14.12.1991 – 13.2.1992	Herd & Mackenzie, Buckie (R)

13.2.1992 – 14.2.1992	Passage to Dumbarton (by road)
14.2.1992 – 25.2.1992	Mcalisters Yard, Dumbarton (ER)
25.2.1992 – 27.2.1992	Passage to Port Erin
27.2.1992 – 7.6.1992	Port Erin (relieving ON.998: 3/1)
7.6.1992 – 8.6.1992	Passage to Dumbarton
8.6.1992 – 17.6.1992	Mcalisters Yard, Dumbarton (ER)
17.6.1992 – 18.6.1992	Passage to Poole
18.6.1992 – 13.5.1993	RNLI Depot Poole (ER, to be withdrawn and placed on the sale list)
13.5.1993 – 15.5.1993	RNLI Depot Poole (std, awaiting sale and transportation)

Notable Rescues

On the morning of 21 September 1980, *Horace Clarkson* was launched from Moelfre to the yacht *July Morn*, of Southampton, which had been reported in difficulties, with a broken rudder, 100yds off Llanddona Beach in Red Wharf Bay, Anglesey. The wind was north-easterly, gale force eight, and the sea was rough with a medium to heavy swell.

After launching under the command of Coxswain Will Roberts, the lifeboat headed towards the casualty, but could not establish direct radio communication. When the yacht was found barely under control with waves breaking over her, Coxswain Roberts decided to try to take the yacht in tow rather than take off her two crew, who were exhausted. After approaching the casualty, Second Coxswain John Thomas was put on board and he took a towline with him. Once on board, the second coxswain made the towline fast and the lifeboat began the tow, heading east towards Puffin Sound and the shelter of the Menai Straits.

Despite constant attention, the tow rope parted eleven times in the three and a half miles from the start of the tow until the two boats finally passed through Puffin Sound. The second coxswain was exposed to the full force of the sea many times, and was nearly washed overboard on several occasions. Each time the tow parted, a considerable degree of seamanship was needed to manoeuvre the lifeboat into a position to reattach it.

Although visibility improved during the morning, the gale continued unabated and only in the relative shelter of the Menai Straits did the situation improve for both rescuers and rescued. The yacht was left at moorings near Menai Bridge after Coxswain Roberts had satisfied himself that her crew needed no more help.

For this service, framed letters signed by the Duke of Atholl, Chairman of the Institution, were sent to Coxswain Roberts and Second Coxswain Thomas. A letter signed by the RNLI Director, Rear Admiral W.J. Graham, was sent to the remainder of the crew for their determination and effort.

Disposal

Horace Clarkson was sold on 13 May 1993 to a buyer based in Hampshire. She was launched on 15 May from the RNLI Depot, Poole, and sailed by the new owner to Southampton, where she arrived later the same day. During the 1990s she was kept moored on the River Itchen below Northam Bridge, Southampton and, unaltered, kept in use as a pleasure boat.

Alice Upjohn

Official Number	1048
Operational Number	37-35
Year built	1977
Builder	William Osborne, Littlehampton
Yard No.	WO 1119
Cost	£130,000
Donor	Gift of Miss Ursula M. Upjohn.
Named	9 October 1978 at Dungeness by Miss Ursula Upjohn in memory of her mother.

Stations

Dungeness	Sept. 1977 – Sept. 1992	147/45

Movements

1.1.1976 – 21.9.1977	William Osborne, Littlehampton (uc; remained at Osbornes for trials until 21.9.77, then to Dungeness)

Alice Upjohn outside the lifeboat house on her carriage ready to be launched for Lifeboat Day, August 1992. (Paul Russell)

Alice Upjohn being launched at Dungeness on 16 August 1992 for the station's Lifeboat Day. (Paul Russell)

Alice Upjohn outside the lifeboat house at Dungeness in May 1992. (Mark Roberts)

21.9.1977 – 23.9.1977	Passage trials (left Littlehampton on 21.9.77, arrived at Newhaven on same day, Dover on 22.9.77 and Dungeness on 23.9.77)
23.9.1977 – 17.11.1977	Dungeness (CT)
17.11.1977 – 11.9.1981	Dungeness (sl; ON.937 remained at Dungeness to 27.1.79; ON.1048 became fully operational on 17.11.78)
11.9.1981 – 25.3.1982	William Osborne, Littlehampton (rlvd by ON.984)
25.3.1982 – 26.3.1982	Passage to Dungeness
26.3.1982 – 21.12.1987	Dungeness (sl)
21.12.1987 – 15.5.1988	Cantell's Bt Yd, Newhaven (S, rlvd by ON.1047)
15.5.1988 – 25.4.1991	Dungeness (sl)
25.4.1991 – 2.8.1991	Cantell's Bt Yd, Newhaven (S, rlvd by ON.1047)
2.8.1991 – 18.1.1992	Dungeness (sl)
18.1.1992 – 5.2.1992	Cantell's Bt Yd, Newhaven (S, rlvd by ON.1046)
5.2.1992 – 24.9.1992	Dungeness (sl)
24.9.1992 – 28.9.1992	Dungeness (withdrawn after new lifeboat ON.1186 on station, awaiting passage from Dungeness)
28.9.1992 – 29.9.1992	Passage to Otterham Quay
29.9.1992 – 16.2.1994	Crescent Shipyard, Otterham Quay (ER, std for sale from 31.12.1993)
16.2.1994 – 2.5.1995	RNLI Depot, Poole (std for sale from 17.2.1994)

Disposal

Alice Upjohn was sold out of service in May 1995. She was transported overnight from RNLI Depot, Poole, to Tilbury Dock, destined for New Zealand, where she had been purchased by the West Buller Marine SAR Volunteer Coastguard Inc. for use as a rescue boat. In New Zealand, she was renamed *Ivan Talley Rescue* and was escorted into Nelson Harbour by another former RNLI lifeboat, a 33ft Brede. She completed a 350-mile passage from Wellington to her new base at Greymouth, with calls at Nelson and Westport. She saw service before even arriving at her home port, having taken part in a search for a missing fisherman in Westport.

Alice Upjohn being recovered on the steeply sloping shingle beach at Dungeness in August 1991.
(Tony Denton)

Shoreline

Official Number	1054
Operational Number	37-36
Year built	1979
Builder	William Osborne, Littlehampton
Yard No.	WO 1666
Cost	£210,000
Donor	Special Appeal to Shoreline members in 1977-1978.
Named	20 October 1979 at Dun Cow Quay, Blyth, by Sir Alec Rose.

Stations

Blyth	Sept. 1979 – Oct. 1982	12/1
Arbroath	Dec. 1982 – Aug. 1993	39/5

Movements

1.1.1978 – 9.4.1979	Wm Osborne, Littlehampton (uc)
9.4.1979 – 14.8.1979	Wm Osborne, Littlehampton (T)
14.8.1979 – 14.8.1979	Wm Osborne, Littlehampton (final T)
14.8.1979 – 25.8.1979	Wm Osborne, Littlehampton (I)
25.8.1979 – 1.9.1979	Passage to Blyth
1.9.1979 – 18.9.1979	Blyth (CT)
18.9.1979 – 26.10.1982	Blyth (sl)
26.10.1982 – 28.10.1982	Blyth (withdrawn; remained at station after new sl ON.1079 at Blyth)
28.10.1982 – 30.10.1982	Passage to Buckie
30.10.1982 – 11.12.1982	Jones' Yard, Buckie (S, I, re-allocated to Arbroath)

11.12.1982 – 13.12.1982	Passage (CT)
13.12.1982 – 17.12.1982	Arbroath (CT)
17.12.1982 – 21.3.1988	Arbroath (sl)
21.3.1988 – 8.7.1988	Herd & Mackenzie, Buckie (S, rlvd by ON.1022)
8.7.1988 – 9.7.1988	Passage to Arbroath
9.7.1988 – 27.9.1991	Arbroath (sl)
27.9.1991 – 29.9.1991	Passage to Buckie (rlvd by ON.1047 which arrived at Arbroath 22.9.1991)
29.9.1991 – 29.11.1991	Herd & Mackenzie, Buckie (S, rlvd by ON.1047)
29.11.1991 – 30.11.1991	Passage to Arbroath

Shoreline on the slipway at Blyth on 29 March 1980 being recovered after her first service call. (David Phillipson)

Shoreline outside the lifeboat house on the slipway at Blyth in September 1981. (Tony Denton)

Shoreline at Arbroath, with D class ILB to left and the lifeboat house behind. (From a postcard in the author's collection)

30.11.1991 – 26.8.1993	Arbroath (sl, arrived under tow of Montrose lifeboat)
26.8.1993 – 8.9.1993	Arbroath (sl. withdrawn when new sl ON.1194 at station; afloat as ER)
8.9.1993 – 9.9.1993	Passage to RNLI Depot, Poole
9.9.1993 – 28.2.1994	RNLI Depot, Poole (std, for sale)

Notable Rescues

Shoreline's first service launch at Blyth took place on 29 March 1980. She put out three minutes after the inshore lifeboat D-210 had been launched following reports that a sail training vessel had capsized off Blyth harbour in choppy seas and a force six wind. Six youths and an instructor were on board.

The Blyth ILB arrived on the scene first and five youths clinging to the upturned hull were quickly rescued. The sixth youth and instructor had been picked up by another yacht which had been passing. Once *Shoreline* arrived on the scene she began to attempt to take the capsized training boat in tow. With the assistance of the ILB, a tow was secured and the casualty was taken into Blyth harbour at 6.30 p.m.

For this service, a Letter of Appreciation, signed by Commander Bruce Cairns, Chief of Operations, was sent via the station Honorary Secretary to the crews of both lifeboats for their efforts. In addition, the Nautical School, to whom the sail training vessel belonged, sent a letter of thanks to the RNLI commending the seamanship and sound common sense shown by the lifeboatmen during the service.

Disposal

Shoreline was sold on 14 February 1994 to a buyer in Wigtownshire. She was taken from RNLI Depot, Poole, on 24 March 1994 by road to Portpatrick, arriving on 25 March. Renamed *Porta Maggie* and kept in Portpatrick harbour, she was owned locally and was used for fishing charters. By 1995, she was for sale again but has remained at Portpatrick, unaltered, in use as trip boat.

Duke of Kent

Official Number	1055
Operational Number	37–37
Year built	1979
Builder	William Osborne, Littlehampton
Yard No.	WO 1667
Cost	£210,000
Donor	Eastbourne Lifeboat Appeal and special efforts of branches and guilds throughout the country.
Named	3 July 1979 outside the Wish Tower Lifeboat Museum, Eastbourne, by HRH Duke of Kent, President of the RNLI.

Stations

Eastbourne	Apr. 1979 – Aug. 1993	353/86

Movements

1.1.1978 – 21.4.1979	Wm Osborne, Littlehampton (uc)
21.4.1979	Wm Osborne, Littlehampton (capsize and machinery trials)
21.4.1979 – 25.4.1979	Wm Osborne, Littlehampton (passage and forty-hour trials)

Duke of Kent approaching the beach at Eastbourne. (Jeff Morris)

Duke of Kent returning to Eastbourne after service to the motor vessel *Breydon,* 24 February 1991. (Paul Russell)

Duke of Kent off Eastbourne. (From a postcard in the author's collection)

25.4.1979 – 26.4.1979	Eastbourne (slipway trials)
26.4.1979 – 17.6.1979	Eastbourne (sl)
17.6.1979 – 6.7.1979	Cantell's Bt Yd, Newhaven (rlvd by ON.948)
6.7.1979 – 4.7.1983	Eastbourne (sl)
4.7.1983 – 29.10.1983	Wm Osborne, Littlehampton (S, rlvd by ON.948)
29.10.1983 – 17.12.1988	Eastbourne (sl)
17.12.1988 – 26.5.1989	Cantell's Bt Yd, Newhaven (rlvd by ON.1064)

26.5.1989 – 2.8.1992	Eastbourne (sl)
2.8.1992 – 21.10.1992	Cantell's Bt Yd, Newhaven (S, rlvd by ON.1064)
21.10.1992 – 26.11.1992	Eastbourne (sl)
26.11.1992 – 19.12.1992	Cantell's Bt Yd, Newhaven (R, rlvd by ON.1064)
19.12.1992 – 19.7.1993	Eastbourne (sl)
19.7.1993 – 14.8.1993	Eastbourne (ER after new sl ON.1195 on station)
14.8.1993 – 15.8.1993	Passage to Poole
15.8.1993 – 19.7.1995	RNLI Depot, Poole (std, for sale)
19.7.1995 – 20.7.1995	Sold and taken by road to Tayport

Notable Rescues

On 14 April 1991 *Duke of Kent* was launched from Eastbourne to assist in the search for two boats missing in the English Channel. In the storm force winds and heavy seas, a total of seven lifeboats were called out to look for the boats. The Eastbourne crew were at sea for six hours in bitterly cold winds and heavy seas until the search was called off at 4.22 p.m. when the boat they were searching for was spotted capsized, twenty-six miles off Hastings. Although this was assessed as 'no service', a letter signed by the Chief of Operation, Commodore George Cooper, was sent to Coxswain/Mechanic David Corke and the crew for their part in the search.

Duke of Kent performed another noteworthy service on 9 November 1992 when she went to the assistance of the yacht *Gulmaid*, of Rye, which had anchored off Eastbourne in deteriorating conditions. The single man on board had had very little sleep and no food for three days. At 7.15 p.m. the lifeboat was launched under the command of Coxswain/Mechanic David Corke into heavy surf that was pounding the beach. Extra hands were needed to help with the launch but the lifeboat got away safely and headed out through the broken water.

The situation quickly deteriorated when the casualty was hit by a large wave which knocked it over and snapped the anchor rope. With the yacht drifting rapidly towards the shore, Coxswain Corke acted quickly. He took the lifeboat towards the yacht, which was by now only 100yds from the beach. On the second approach the lifeboat was held alongside the yacht's starboard side long enough for the lifeboatmen to grab the yachtsman and pull him on board the lifeboat. By this time, the two vessels were only 80yds from the beach, and after the lifeboat backed away into deeper water the yacht went ashore on the beach. The shore team had to ensure the casualty did not block the lifeboat's recovery ramp, and so used a winch to secure it on the beach and enabling the lifeboat to be recovered safely.

For this service, a Letter of Thanks signed by the Director, Lt-Com. Brian Miles, was sent to Coxswain Corke and the lifeboat crew, plus the head launcher, John Delaney, and all the shore helpers, for a 'fine display of teamwork, both on board the lifeboat and ashore'.

Disposal

Duke of Kent was sold on 19 July 1995 and taken to Tayport, on the north bank of the River Tay; she arrived at her new home on 20 July. She was left unaltered and was used as a survey boat on the River Tay, sometimes operating out of the Victoria Dock in Dundee. Since the late 1990s she has been out of the water at Tayport.

Princess of Wales

Official Number	1063
Operational Number	37-38
Year built	1981
Builder	William Osborne, Littlehampton
Yard No.	WO 2091
Cost	£239,197
Donor	The Welsh Lifeboat Appeal to commemorate the marriage of HRH the Prince of Wales and Lady Diana Spencer in 1981, together with other gifts and legacies.
Named	25 November 1982 at Barmouth by HRH the Princess of Wales.

Stations

Barmouth	Mar. 1982 – Oct. 1992	36/8
Relief	1992 – 1993	0/0

Movements

Originally allocated to Aldeburgh; after trials programme re-allocated to Barmouth.

7.10.1981 – 20.3.1982	Wm Osborne, Littlehampton (uc, T)
28.10.1981 – 30.10.1981	Initial trials programme, SR T
2.11.1981 – 30.11.1981	Self-righting trials programme started, then hauled up for machinery trials
1.12.1981 – 15.12.1981	Littlehampton (T)
11.3.1982 – 20.3.1982	Final trials and pass out ready to sail
20.3.1982 – 25.3.1982	Passage to Barmouth (CT)
25.3.1982 – 26.3.1982	Barmouth
26.3.1982 – 1.11.1982	Barmouth (sl)

Princess of Wales leaves Barmouth on 24 September 1992 to meet her replacement, 12m Mersey *Moira Barrie* (ON.1185). (Jeff Morris)

Princess of Wales on exercise at Barmouth on 16 September 1990, with the viaduct in the background. (Tony Denton)

1.11.1982 – 9.11.1982	Anglesey Bt Yd, Beaumaris (S, rlvd by ON.967)
9.11.1982 – 17.4.1983	Barmouth (sl)
17.4.1983 – 10.6.1983	Anglesey Bt Yd, Beaumaris (rlvd by ON.967)
10.6.1983 – 18.11.1984	Barmouth (sl)
18.11.1984 – 20.2.1985	Anglesey Bt Yd, Beaumaris (rlvd by ON.967)
20.2.1985 – 15.3.1986	Barmouth (sl)
15.3.1986 – 26.5.1986	Bangor Shipyard, Northern Ireland (rlvd by ON.967)
26.5.1986 – 31.5.1987	Barmouth (sl)
31.5.1987 – 28.7.1987	Anglesey Bt Yd, Beaumaris (S, rlvd by ON.967)
28.7.1987 – 2.8.1987	Anglesey Bt Yd, Beaumaris (T)
2.8.1987 – 15.2.1989	Barmouth (sl)
15.2.1989 – 10.4.1989	Barmouth (sl, T out of Barmouth periodically and moored at Port Dinorwic Dock)
10.4.1989 – 1.9.1989	Anglesey Bt Yd, Beaumaris (S, rlvd by ON.1022)
1.9.1989 – 8.10.1990	Barmouth (sl)
8.10.1990 – 19.1.1991	Anglesey Bt Yd, Beaumaris (S, rlvd by ON.1022)
21.1.1991 – 16.1.1992	Barmouth (sl)
16.1.1992 – 18.3.1992	Anglesey Bt Yd, Beaumaris (S, rlvd by ON.1022, passage to Beaumaris overnight 15-16.1.1992)
18.3.1992 – 7.10.1992	Barmouth (sl)
7.10.1992 – 17.10.1992	Barmouth (withdrawn with new sl at Barmouth ON.1185; ER at station awaiting passage to Poole)
17.10.1992 – 22.10.1992	Passage to Poole
22.10.1992 – 18.5.1993	RNLI Depot, Poole (ER and std, to be placed on the sale list)

Princess of Wales lies at her moorings at Barmouth on 31 August 1991. (Paul Russell)

Disposal

Princess of Wales was sold out of service on 18 May 1993 and taken to be owned in Portsmouth, Hampshire. She was renamed *Glow Worm*, registered at Portsmouth, and kept unaltered at Port Solent Village Marina, Portsmouth.

The Davys Family

Official Number	1064
Operational Number	37–39
Year built	1981
Builder	William Osborne, Littlehampton
Yard No.	WO 2092
Cost	£240,000
Donor	Gift from Mrs A.E. Mason in memory of the William Davys family.
Named	21 August 1981 at Kingston Beach, Shoreham, by HRH Princess Alexandra of Kent.

Stations

Shoreham Harbour	Aug. 1981 – July 1986	58/16
Relief	1986 – 1993	27*/6

*Including a passage service undertaken on 1.9.1990 to the yacht *Kellog*, gave help.

Movements

21.8.1981 – 16.7.1986	Shoreham Harbour (sl)
19.7.1986 – 19.12.1986	Cantell's Bt Yd, Newhaven (S, withdrawn from Shoreham and placed into Relief)
21.12.1986 – 7.4.1988	Sennen Cove (rlvg ON.999: 4/0)
10.4.1988 – 17.12.1988	Cantell's Bt Yd, Newhaven (S)
17.12.1988 – 26.5.1989	Eastbourne (rlvg ON.1055: 3/0)
26.5.1989 – –30.5.1989	Newhaven Marina (std)
30.5.1989 – 31.5.1989	Passage to Aldeburgh
31.5.1989 – 7.9.1989	Aldeburgh (rlvg ON.1068: 2/0)
7.9.1989 – 18.2.1990	Walmer (rlvg ON.1024: 6/0)
18.2.1990 – 19.2.1990	Passage to Rochester
19.2.1990 – 1.9.1990	Denton Shiprepairers Ltd, Otterham Quay (S)
1.9.1990 – 1.9.1990	Passage to Aldeburgh (1/0)
1.9.1990 – 17.11.1990	Aldeburgh (rlvg ON.1068)
17.11.1990 – 23.5.1991	Denton Shiprepairers Ltd, Otterham Quay (std)
23.5.1991 – 23.5.1991	Passage to Swanage (by road)
23.5.1991 – 6.8.1991	Swanage (rlvg ON.1023: 6/2)
6.8.1991 – 19.8.1991	RNLI Depot, Poole (Depot relief)
19.8.1991 – 17.1.1992	Fletchers Bt Yd, Lowestoft (S)
17.1.1992 – 14.4.1992	Denton Shiprepairers Ltd, Otterham Quay (std, ER)
14.4.1992 – 24.6.1992	Aldeburgh (rlvg ON.1068: 1/0)
24.6.1992 – 1.8.1992	Denton Shiprepairers Ltd, Otterham Quay (std)
1.8.1992 – 2.8.1992	Passage to Eastbourne
2.8.1992 – 21.10.1992	Eastbourne (rlvg ON.1055: 4/4)
21.10.1992 – 28.10.1992	Newhaven Marina (awaiting passage)
28.10.1992 – 29.10.1992	Passage to Otterham Quay

The *Davys Family* moored in the harbour at Shoreham. (David Gooch)

29.10.1992 – 26.11.1992	Denton Shiprepairers Ltd, Otterham Quay (ER)
26.11.1992 – 20.12.1992	Eastbourne (rlvg ON.1055, to Newhaven for ER: 0/0)
20.12.1992 – 2.3.1994	Denton Shiprepairers Ltd, Otterham Quay (std, ER)
2.3.1994 – 3.3.1994	Passage to Poole (by road)
3.3.1994 – 16.1.1996	RNLI Depot, Poole (std for disposal)

The Davys Family at Walmer while on relief duty there, September 1989. (Mark Roberts)

The Davys Family launching on exercise at Eastbourne on 8 January 1989 while on relief duty there. (Paul Russell)

Notable Rescues

On 9 December 1982, *The Davys Family* was launched from Shoreham Harbour at 9.36 p.m. under Coxswain Kenneth Everard to the cargo vessel *Andoni*, of Panama, which had suffered engine failure two and a half miles south of Shoreham. Newhaven's 44ft Waveney *Louis Marchesi of Round Table* (ON.1045) was also launched and the tug *Meeching* was alerted.

The two lifeboats rendezvoused at 10.10 p.m. and stood by the casualty while a tow rope was passed between it and the tug. After some difficulty, the tow was finally connected at 11.58 p.m., by which time *Andoni* was dangerously close to going ashore at Old Nore, a mile west of Newhaven.

While standing by in the very rough seas, one of the Shoreham crew on board *The Davys Family* fell and sustained a head injury. At 12.36 a.m., on 10 December, the lifeboat headed for Newhaven where an ambulance was waiting for the injured crewmember. After he had been landed and three more crew members had been taken on board, the lifeboat returned to the scene and continued to stand by.

By 1.55 a.m. the tug, with *Andoni* in tow, was in safe water three miles offshore, and so the two lifeboats were stood down. For this service, Letters of Appreciation were sent to both the Master of the tug *Meeching* and to Coxswain Everard and the Shoreham crew for their efforts in standing by throughout.

Disposal

The Davys Family was sold out of service in July 1995 to the 2nd Walthamstow Sea Scout Group. She was taken by road to Shepperton Marina on 16 January 1996, from where she went to London Docklands. She was used as a Scout boat based at Canary Wharf, West India Docks, and renamed *The Martin Family*. In 1998 she was on the River Crouch, but returned to the West India Docks, where she is kept opposite Meridian Gates.

James Cable

Official Number	1068
Operational Number	37–40
Year built	1981
Builder	William Osborne, Littlehampton
Yard No.	WO 2222
Cost	£246,000
Donor	Funded from the proceeds of the Aldeburgh Lifeboat Appeal, and various other sources, named in memory of one of Aldeburgh's most famous coxswains.
Named	20 September 1982 at Aldeburgh by HRH the Duke of Kent.

Stations

Aldeburgh	June 1982 – Nov. 1993	54/24

James Cable is launched over the beach at the end of her naming ceremony in September 1982.
(Jeff Morris)

Movements

9.6.1979 – 26.1.1982	Wm Osborne, Littlehampton (uc)
26.1.1982 – 29.1.1982	Self-righting trials programme
29.1.1982 – 1.3.1982	Hauled up following trials
1.3.1982 – 17.3.1982	Initial trials programme
17.3.1982 – 25.5.1982	Hauled up following trials
25.5.1982 – 5.6.1982	Final trials programme
5.6.1982 – 7.6.1982	Passage to Aldeburgh
7.6.1982 – 3.11.1983	Aldeburgh (sl)
3.11.1983 – 9.2.1984	Whisstocks Yard, Woodbridge (rlvd by ON.948)
9.2.1984 – 25.10.1984	Aldeburgh (sl)
25.10.1984 – 10.11.1984	Whisstocks Yard, Woodbridge (rlvd by ON.948)
10.11.1984 – 15.2.1985	Aldeburgh (sl)
15.2.1985 – 13.4.1985	Whisstocks Yard, Woodbridge (rlvd by ON.948)
13.4.1985 – 1.2.1986	Aldeburgh (sl)
1.2.1986 – 4.7.1987	Brown's Bt Yd, Rowhedge (rlvd by ON.948)
4.7.1987 – 24.11.1987	Aldeburgh (sl)
24.11.1987 – 24.11.1987	Local slipway (M)
24.11.1987 – 10.5.1988	Aldeburgh (sl)
10.5.1988 – 10.5.1988	Local slipway (R)
10.5.1988 – 31.5.1989	Aldeburgh (sl)
31.5.1989 – 7.9.1989	Fletchers Bt Yd, Lowestoft (S, rlvd by ON.1064)
7.9.1989 – 1.9.1990	Aldeburgh (sl)
1.9.1990 – 17.11.1990	Fletchers Bt Yd, Lowestoft (S, rlvd by ON.1064)

17.11.1990 – 14.4.1992	Aldeburgh (sl)
14.4.1992 – 24.6.1992	Fletchers Bt Yd, Lowestoft (S, rlvd by ON.1064)
24.6.1992 – 6.9.1993	Aldeburgh (sl)
6.9.1993 – 7.9.1993	Hull clean and antifoul in preparation for lying afloat in River Alde
7.9.1993 – 20.12.1993	Aldeburgh (sl, afloat in River Alde during boathouse construction)
20.12.1993 – 11.1.1994	Titchmarsh Marine, Walton (std, awaiting passage to Poole)
11.1.1994 – 1.5.1994	Passage by road to RNLI Depot, Poole (std from 18.1.1994)
1.5.1994 – 7.7.1995	RNLI Depot, Poole (sold to ADES, Uruguay, but std at Depot)
7.7.1995 – 8.7.1995	Passage by road to Tilbury for shipment to Uruguay
8.7.1995	At Tilbury Docks to be loaded and shipped to Uruguay

Notable Rescues

On 24 October 1984, *James Cable* was launched from Aldeburgh beach at 2.02 p.m. to a Rig Platform Unit off Sizewell Nuclear Power Station. Conditions had been deteriorating all morning and a southerly gale was blowing by the time the lifeboat was at sea. The lifeboat headed north at full speed and reached the platform twenty-five minutes after launching. Twelve maintenance men were on board the platform and the lifeboat was to take them off.

James Cable on the cradle at the head of the beach at Aldeburgh. (Jeff Morris)

Coxswain Billy Burrell approached the platform where the confused sea and a heavy swell made conditions particularly difficult. However, it was impossible to get the lifeboat alongside as steel girders were jutting out from the platform. So the coxswain went in bow first, and managed to take off one of the men before backing away. The second approach had to be rapidly aborted when a sudden heavy sea swept the lifeboat towards the platform.

On the third run-in two men jumped on board as Coxswain Burrell held the lifeboat in position by skilful use of the engines and rudder. However, a following sea lifted the lifeboat and jammed her bows under one of the steel projections. The boat suffered some damage but fortunately the two lifeboatmen in the bow were uninjured. The lifeboat was brought clear and another run was made. This time, eight men jumped off the platform, one sustaining serious injuries to his leg when he landed in the lifeboat.

There was still one man remaining on the platform, so another run had to be made. The man was very reluctant to jump but eventually he was dragged aboard by the lifeboatman and Coxswain Burrell was able to take the lifeboat clear and head back to Aldeburgh. Heavy seas repeatedly swept the lifeboat as she headed south into the huge waves. It took half an hour to reach her station, where she was beached at 3.10 p.m. The injured man was taken to hospital and the lifeboat safely recovered.

For this service, a Letter of Appreciation signed by the Chief of Operations, Com. Bruce Cairns, was sent to Coxswain Burrell and the crew for their efforts.

Disposal

James Cable was sold in July 1994 to ADES, the Uruguay Lifeboat Association, to continue to serve as a lifeboat. She was taken from RNLI Depot, Poole, to Tilbury Docks for passage to Uruguay in July 1995. Once in Uruguay, she was renamed *Ades 13 Augustin Carlevaro* and was stationed at Puerto de Carmelo.

Replacement Summary

Op No.	Station*	Launch	First replaced by	Present
37–01	Scarborough	Carriage	Oakley (37–12)	Mersey
37–02	Sheringham	Carriage	Oakley (37–19)	Atlantic 75
37–03	Weston-super-Mare	Slipway	McLachlan	Atlantic 75
37–04	Boulmer	Carriage	Station closed	PLB
	Filey	Carriage	Mersey	Mersey
37–05	Seaham harbour	Slipway	Station closed	–
	Flamborough	Skids	Atlantic 21	Atlantic 75
37–06	Hastings	Carriage	Mersey	Mersey
37–07	St Abbs	Slipway	D class inflatable	Atlantic 75
	Newcastle	Carriage	Oakley (37–01) TSD	Mersey
37–08	Cullercoats	Carriage	D class inflatable	Atlantic 21
	Redcar	Carriage	Atlantic 21	Atlantic 75
37–09	Llandudno	Carriage	Mersey	Mersey

37–10	Skegness	Carriage	Mersey	Mersey
37–11	Caister-on-Sea	Carriage	Station closed	PLB
	Runswick	Carriage	Station closed	PLB
	Pwllheli	Carriage	Mersey	Mersey
37–12	Scarborough	Carriage	Mersey	Mersey
37–13	Cromer No.2	Carriage	Station closed	–
	Bridlington	Carriage	Mersey	Mersey
37–14	Kirkcudbright	Slipway	Atlantic 21	Atlantic 21
37–15	Wells-next-the-Sea	Carriage	Mersey	Mersey
37–16	Anstruther	Carriage	Mersey	Mersey
37–17	Newbiggin	Carriage	Atlantic 21	Atlantic 75
37–18	Clacton-on-Sea	Slipway	Atlantic 21	Atlantic 75
	Clogher Head	Carriage	Oakley (37–01) TSD	Mersey
37–19	Ilfracombe	Carriage	Mersey	Mersey
37–20	North Sunderland	Carriage	Oakley (37–13) TSD	Mersey
37–21	St Ives	Carriage	Oakley (37–06) TSD	Mersey
37–22	Rhyl	Carriage	Rother	Mersey
37–23	Relief only	–	–	–
37–24	Ramsey (IOM)	Carriage	Mersey	Mersey
37–25	New Quay	Carriage	Oakley (37–06) TSD	Mersey
37–26	Kilmore Quay	Carriage	Oakley (37–23) TSD	Mersey
37–27	Port Erin	Slipway	Atlantic 21	Atlantic 21
37–28	Sennen Cove	Slipway	Mersey	47ft Tyne
37–29	Hoylake	Carriage	Mersey	Mersey
	Rhyl	Carriage	Rother	Mersey
37–30	Amble	Afloat	Waveney	Mersey
37–31	Swanage	Slipway	Mersey	Mersey
37–32	Walmer	Skids	Atlantic 21	Atlantic 21
37–33	Margate	Carriage	Mersey	Mersey
37–34	Moelfre	Slipway	46ft 9in Watson motor	47ft Tyne
37–35	Dungeness	Carriage	Mersey	Mersey
37–36	Blyth	Slipway	Waveney	14m Trent
	Arbroath	Slipway	Mersey	Mersey
37–37	Eastbourne	Skids	Mersey	Mersey
37–38	Barmouth	Afloat	Mersey	Mersey
37–39	Shoreham Harbour	Slipway	47ft Watson motor	47ft Tyne
37–40	Aldeburgh	Skids	Mersey	Mersey

★ Only stations which operated an Oakley/Rother as station boat are listed

PLB – private lifeboat established

TSD – temporary station duty

3

After service

Taken out of service

The first Oakley was built in 1958 and the last Rother completed in 1982, a construction programme spanning more than two decades. Throughout this time, the concept
behind the design remained basically unchanged and it was as effective in the 1990s
as it was in the 1950s. But times were changing, and as the RNLI's quest for speed
was stepped up in the 1980s so the Oakleys and Rothers were gradually superseded
by faster lifeboats. The Institution intended to have 'fast' lifeboats at every all–weather
station by the end of 1993, and in November of that year the last of the Rothers,
stationed at Aldeburgh, was taken out of service. The Oakleys and Rothers were
gradually sold out of service or disposed of, many Oakleys becoming museum pieces
at various places throughout the country. Two went to the Lifeboat Collection at
Chatham Historic Dockyard. Most of the Rothers remained afloat and in use, some
being sent abroad for use as lifeboats with foreign lifeboat societies. This chapter
describes what happened to the Oakleys and Rothers after their RNLI service.

Ernest Tom Neathercoat on display outside the International Boat Building Centre at Oulton Broad,
Lowestoft, in June 1994. (Nicholas Leach)

After Service Summary

37–01   Displayed as part of the Lifeboat Collection, Chatham Historic Dockyard, Kent.

37–02   Displayed at Muckleburgh Collection, Weybourne, then stored at Aylsham prior to going to Sheringham for display inside lifeboat museum.

37–03   Displayed at Milford Haven Docks, Pembrokeshire.

37–04   Sold to Nuclear Electric and displayed at Hartlepool, Cleveland, used as a travelling exhibit for fund-raising purposes.

37–05   Displayed as part of the Lifeboat Collection, Chatham Historic Dockyard, Kent.

37–06   Sold at Norwich 1995, moved to Blakeney, Norfolk, used as a pleasure boat.

37–07   Broken up at Arklow Marine & Leisure Ltd, Arklow, 1995.

37–08   Displayed at Old Hall Museum, Kirkleatham, near Redcar, Cleveland.

37–09   Stored at Verolme Shipyard, Cork, then moved to Cobh for conversion.

37–10   Broken up at Branksea Marine, Wareham, Dorset, 1993.

37–11   Sold at Norwich 1995, and stored at Hewitt's Bt Yd, Blakeney, Norfolk.

37–12   Displayed at Shipwreck & Heritage Museum, Charlestown, Cornwall.

37–13   Hull gutted and used as a climbing frame at Childrens Culture Centre, Arvon Road, London.

37–14   Displayed outside Baytree Garden Centre, Weston, Spalding, Lincolnshire.

37–15   Displayed at International Boatbuilding Training Centre, Oulton Broad, Lowestoft, later moved to Wells-next-the-Sea for display there.

37–16   Displayed at the Drifter Centre, Buckie, Banffshire.

37–17   Displayed at Child-Beale Wildlife Trust, near Reading, Berkshire.

37–18   Displayed at Lifeboat Museum, The Green, Harwich, Essex.

37–19   Broken up at Otterham Quay, Kent, 1992.

37–20   Broken up at Belsize Bt Yd, Southampton, 1989.

37–21   Broken up at Belsize Bt Yd, Southampton, 1989.

37–22   Displayed at the Marine Life Centre, St Davids, Pembrokeshire.

37–23   Broken up at Arklow Marine & Leisure Ltd, Arklow, 1995.

37–24   Broken up at McAllister's Bt Yd, Dumbarton, 1992.

37–25   Displayed at the Sea Watch Centre, Moelfre, Anglesey.

37–26   Broken up at Arklow Marine & Leisure Ltd, Arklow, 1995.

37–27   Sold to become a lifeboat in Estonia, renamed *Anita* and stationed at Haapsalu, on the western coast of Estonia.

37–28   Sold 1992 to Sumner Lifeboat Institution, New Zealand, to become lifeboat *Joseph Day*, stationed at Sumner 1992 to 1999, then sold to private owner.

37–29   Used as a pleasure boat at Nene Park, Peterborough, until 2000 when she was given to Chatham Historic Dockyard for use as a floating exhibit.

37–30   Sold 1992, renamed *TSMV Salvesen* and kept at the River Tawe Marina; moved to Bristol, and by 2000 was at Instow on the River Torridge, Devon.

37–31   Sold in 1995, used as a pleasure boat at Chichester Marina, renamed *Louise*.

37-32   Sold in 1992, unaltered at Monkston Marina, Swansea, subsequently
           moved to Plymouth.
37-33   Sold in March 1994 and became a pleasure boat at East Ferry, Cork;
           later moved to Skibbereen and in 2002 to Shannon harbour.
37-34   Sold in May 1993, kept on the River Itchen at Southampton,
           unaltered.
37-35   Sold in 1995 to West Coast Buller Marine, New Zealand, for use as a
           rescue boat, renamed *Ivan Talley Rescue* and operated from Greymouth.
37-36   Sold in 1994, renamed *Porta Maggie*, and operated out of Portpatrick.
37-37   Used as a survey boat and kept at Tayport, opposite Broughty Ferry.
37-38   Sold 1993, renamed *Glow Worm*; kept at Port Solent Village Marina,
           unaltered as a pleasure boat, but sold in 2000 and moved to Skibbereen,
           Co. Cork.
37-39   Sold to the London Sea Scouts, and kept at West India Docks, London;
           used as a Scout boat, renamed *The Martin Family*.
37-40   Sold out of service to Uruguay for use as a lifeboat at Montevideo,
           renamed *Ades 13 Augustin Carlevaro*.

Note: further details can be found in the entries for the individual boats.

J.G. Graves of Sheffield, the prototype 37ft Oakley, on display as part of the lifeboat collection at
Chatham Historic Dockyard. (Nicholas Leach)

The Sheringham lifeboat for almost thirty years, *The Manchester Unity of Oddfellows* on display at Weybourne, Norfolk, in August 1994 together with *J.C. Madge* (to right, out of picture), another former Sheringham lifeboat. (Nicholas Leach)

Calouste Gulbenkain on display outside the local museum at Milford Haven Docks in August 1996. (Nicholas Leach)

Robert and Dorothy Hardcastle at Hartlepool on the low loader used to transport her around the country to fund-raising events. (Nicholas Leach)

The Will and Fanny Kirby inside the covered slips at Chatham Historic Dockyard as one of the lifeboats on display. (Supplied by Tony Denton)

Fairlight entering the harbour at Wells-next-the-Sea in August 1998 as one of the lifeboats taking part in an ex lifeboat rally organised by Wells lifeboat station to raise funds for the RNLI. *Fairlight* is one of few Oakleys that remain afloat and in use. (Nicholas Leach)

The sad sight of *Jane Hay* being broken up at Arklow in August 1995. She was in a small boatyard with two other Oakleys, 37-23 and 37-26, which were also being dismantled. (Nicholas Leach)

Sir James Knott on display at Kirkleatham Old Hall Museum, near Redcar, Cleveland. (From a photograph supplied by Tony Denton)

Lilly Wainwright at Verolme Dockyard, Cork, in April 2000. Since then, she has been moved and surveyed for use on the Irish inland waterways. (Nicholas Leach)

The Royal Thames out of the water at the RNLI Depot, Poole, prior to disposal. (Paul Russell)

The Royal Thames
out of the water at
Hewitt's Bt Yd,
Blakeney, Norfolk.
(Tony Denton)

Amelia on
display outside
at the
Shipwreck and
Heritage
Museum,
Charlestown,
Cornwall, in
April 1995.
(Nicholas
Leach)

*William Henry
and Mary King* in
store at the RNLI
Depot, Poole, in
December 1990
prior to disposal.
She was
subsequently sent
to the Childrens
Culture Centre at
Drayton Park
School, London.
(Nicholas Leach)

Mary Pullman on display outside Baytree Garden Centre, near Spalding, Lincolnshire, July 1995. She has been stripped of all internal fittings. (Tony Denton)

Ernest Tom Neathercoat on display in the car park at Wells-next-the-Sea, August 1998. She had been displayed at the International Boat Building Centre in Oulton Broad before being brought to Wells in 1998. (Nicholas Leach)

Outside at Buckie Drifter Centre, *The Doctors* on display in August 2002. She had served at Anstruther, one of only three Oakleys that saw service in Scotland, so displaying her in Scotland was particularly appropriate. (Nicholas Leach)

Mary Joicey on display at Child-Beale Wildlife Trust, at Church Farm, Lower Basildon, near Reading, Berkshire. (Peter Edey)

Valentine Wyndham-Quin outside the lifeboat museum at Cromer while on display there. She was subsequently moved to Harwich where she was displayed inside the old lifeboat house as the centrepiece of a small lifeboat museum. (Phil Weeks)

Lloyds II being dismantled and broken up at Crescent Marine, May 1994. (Photograph supplied by Tony Denton)

Frank Penfold Marshall at the RNLI Depot, Poole, awaiting disposal in June 1989. She was broken up later that year in Southampton. (Paul Russell)

After serving at Rhyl for more than two decades, *Har-Lil* is seen on display outside the Marine Life Centre at St Davids, Pembrokeshire, in August 1996. (Nicholas Leach)

The remains of *James Ball Ritchie* after she had been broken up and burned at McAllister's Bt Yd, Dumbarton, February 1993. The last digit of her operational number, 4, can just be made out on the side of her engine casing remains. (R. McLaughlin)

Birds Eye on display at the Sea Watch Centre, Moelfre, Anglesey. She forms the centrepiece of the display in the small museum near the local lifeboat station. (Nicholas Leach)

Lady Murphy at Arklow being broken up in August 1995. She was one of three Oakleys dismantled at this time. (Nicholas Leach)

Osman Gabriel on the quayside at RNLI Depot, Poole, on 8 September 1992 prior to being sold to the Estonian lifeboat service. She was handed over at a ceremony at Tallinn on 18 March 1993 and renamed *Anita* for use as a lifeboat at Haapsula. (David Gooch)

After service with the RNLI, *Diana White* served the Sumner Lifeboat Institution in New Zealand for a number of years. She was renamed *Joseph Day* and this photograph shows her travelling up the Kaiapoi river to attend a naming ceremony at Waimakariri-Ashlay Lifeboat Institute, ten miles north of Sumner. (By courtesy of Walter Baguley)

Diana White was renamed *Joseph Day* for service with the Sumner Lifeboat Institution in New Zealand. This photograph of the Sumner crew, taken on 9 April 1995, shows the boat on the slipway from which she was operated. (By courtesy of Tim Stevens)

After her life-saving service at Sumner ended in 1999, *Joseph Day* was sold into private ownership and her name reverted to *Diana White*. She was used as a pleasure boat based at Taurananga, Bay of Plenty. (By courtesy of Tim Stevens)

Mary Gabriel flies the RNLI flag alongside Thunderbolt Pier, at Chatham Historic
Dockyard, in June 2002. She had been owned by a family from Northamptonshire
who donated her to the National Lifeboat Collection at Chatham in 2001 for use
as a floating exhibit and ambassador for the collection. She arrived at Chatham on
3 June 2001 having been taken from her previous base at Wells by volunteers from
Chatham. (Nicholas Leach)

Harold Salvesen
moored at the
Tawe Marina,
Swansea, in May
1997, renamed
TSMV Salvesen
and unaltered
under private
ownership. She
was refurbished at
Pembroke Dock in
2001-2002 and
moved to Mylor,
Cornwall, in 2002.
(Nicholas Leach)

*J. Reginald
Corah* at
Birdham Pool,
near Chichester,
in July 1997.
(Nicholas
Leach)

J. Reginald Corah at Swanage lifeboat station in July 2002 for the local Lifeboat Day. The bow of the station's 12m Mersey, which replaced her, can just be seen to the left. *J. Reginald Corah* was being used to run trips for holidaymakers as a way of raising money for the RNLI. She is privately owned and had come to Swanage from her usual base at Chichester Marina for the week. (Nicholas Leach)

The Hampshire Rose out of the water at Monkston Marina, near Swansea, in May 1997, with her hull painted yellow. In 2000, she was moved to Plymouth under new ownership, but remained unaltered. (Nicholas Leach)

Silver Jubilee (Civil Service No.33) at Old Court Boatyard near Skibbereen, Co. Cork, April 1999. She was sold out of service to a buyer in Ireland, was renamed *Catherie* and her aft cockpit was extended over the stern. She was later moved to Shannon. (Nicholas Leach)

Horace Clarkson at Vestapian Road, Southampton, in May 1997. She was sold out of service in May 1993 and was taken to the Solent, where she was kept at a berth on the River Itchen and remained largely unaltered. (Tony Denton)

After service, *Alice Upjohn* was sold out of service to West Buller Marine SAR Volunteer Coastguard in New Zealand, and renamed *Ivan Talley Rescue*. She is seen here during trials out of Wellington in July 1995. (V.H. Young & L.A. Sawyer)

After being sold out of service, *Shoreline* was renamed *Porta Maggie*, was kept at Portpatrick and used as a trip boat remaining largely unaltered. This photograph shows her at moorings in the small harbour at Portpatrick. (Nicholas Leach)

Duke of Kent out of the water at Tayport, opposite Dundee, July 2000. She was used as a survey boat immediately after being sold out of service, but has spent several years out of the water. (Nicholas Leach)

Princess of Wales on the quayside at the RNLI Depot, Poole, in July 1993. She was renamed *Glow Worm*, and kept at Portsmouth by private owners before being moved to Skibbereen, Co. Cork. (Tony Denton)

The Davys Family on the quayside at the RNLI Depot, Poole, in October 1994. On 21 July 1995, she was sold to the Walthamstow Sea Scouts, and has been based in London ever since, renamed *The Martin Family*, and kept at West India Docks. (Nicholas Leach)

James Cable out of the water at the RNLI Depot, Poole, in October 1994 before being sold to Uruguay for use as a lifeboat at Montevideo. She was subsequently taken to Tilbury for transportation to Montevideo, Uruguay. (Nicholas Leach)

Stations served by Oakleys and Rothers

ARBROATH
ANSTRUTHER
St ABBS
NORTH SUNDERLAND
BOULMER
AMBLE
NEWBIGGIN
BLYTH
CULLERCOATS
SEAHAM HARBOUR
REDCAR
RUNSWICK
SCARBOROUGH
FILEY
FLAMBOROUGH
BRIDLINGTON

SKEGNESS
WELLS
SHERINGHAM
CROMER

CAISTER

ALDEBURGH

CLACTON-ON-SEA

MARGATE

WALMER

DUNGENESS

HASTINGS

SHOREHAM HARBOUR
EASTBOURNE

SWANAGE

WESTON-SUPER-MARE
ILFRACOMBE

ST IVES
SENNEN COVE

KILMORE QUAY
NEW QUAY
BARMOUTH
PWLLHELI
MOELFRE
LLANDUDNO
RHYL
HOYLAKE
PORT ERIN
RAMSEY
KIRKCUDBRIGHT

NEWCASTLE
CLOGHER HEAD

Bibliography and Further Reading

Cameron, Ian, *Riders of the Storm* (Weidenfeld & Nicolson, London, 2002)

Dutton, Lt-Com. W.L.G., 'A Review of the Royal National Lifeboat Institution's Lifeboats in the Twentieth Century' (Paper No.4 in International Lifeboat Conference *Report*, 1975, XII ILC, pp.63-80)

Fawcett, Ralph, *The Bridlington Lifeboats* (1985)

Fry, Eric, *Lifeboat Design and Development* (David & Charles, 1975)

Leach, Nicholas, *For Those in peril: The Lifeboat Service of the United Kingdom and Republic of Ireland, Station by Station* (Silver Link Publishing, 1999)

— *The Waveney Lifeboats* (Bernard McCall, Portishead, 2001)

Macdonald, S. et al, *RNLI Lifeboats in the 1970s* (Royal Institution of Naval Architects, pp.301-324)

Morris, Jeff, *Lists of British Lifeboats Part 3: Steam Lifeboats 1888-1901 and Motor Lifeboats 1904-1993* (1994)

— *The Story of the Scarborough Lifeboats* (2nd Edition, 1998)

— *The History of Seahouses Lifeboats* (1999)

— *The History of the Rhyl Lifeboats* (1995)

— *The History of the North Deal, Walmer and Kingsdowne Lifeboats* (1999)

Paffett, James, 'Fail Safe, Part 1: Capsizing and Righting' (*The Lifeboat*, Vol.49, Spring 1984, pp.14-15, 19)

Thatcher, Keith, 'Looking at Lifeboats – The Oakley and Rother' (*The Lifeboat*, Vol.53, Spring 1994, pp.156-157)

Welford, Stuart, 'Is it Right to Right?' (*Lifeboat International*, July 1974, pp. 4-16)

Index